MARVELLOUS SYNERGY

PHASE THREE

AN UNOFFICIAL GUIDE TO THE MARVEL CINEMATIC UNIVERSE

Andy Thai

Copyright © Andy Thai 2021

Eureka Enigma Publishing

ISBN 978-0-6451446-2-8

Cover design and typesetting by Andy Thai
Edited by Keelan Judge and Lauren Pearce

This book is an unofficial guide and has not been authorised, endorsed, licensed, or approved by The Walt Disney Company, Marvel Entertainment, Marvel Studios, or any other entities associated with adaptations of Marvel properties. Some words used in the text are property of the trademark holder and have been used for identification purposes only.

All rights reserved. No part of this publication may be reproduced, stored in a retrieval system, or transmitted, in any form or by any means, electronic, mechanical, photocopying, recording or otherwise, without the prior permission of the publisher.

For Stan Lee

CONTENTS

Introduction ... 1

Phase Three
    Captain America: Civil War (2016) ... 5
    Doctor Strange (2016) ... 19
    Guardians of the Galaxy Vol. 2 (2017) ... 33
    Spider-Man: Homecoming (2017) ... 45
    Thor: Ragnarok (2017) ... 61
    Black Panther (2018) ... 75
    Avengers: Infinity War (2018) ... 89
    Ant-Man and the Wasp (2018) ... 105
    Captain Marvel (2019) ... 117
    Avengers: Endgame (2019) ... 131
    Spider-Man: Far From Home (2019) ... 151

Appendices
    List of Infinity Stones ... 167
    The Infinity Saga in Chronological Order ... 169

Acknowledgements ... 173
Bibliography ... 175
Photo Credits ... 181

INTRODUCTION

For me, seeing the "Civil War" story—one of my favourite arcs from the comic books—play out on screen was thrilling to watch. (For those wondering, I'm on Team Cap.) Had 2016's *Captain America: Civil War* been released any earlier, I'm not sure it would have had the same impact. The history between Steve Rogers and Tony Stark, built up over several films, ensures the ending is as heartbreaking as it should be. Moreover, it features a large cast of characters—many of whom were already familiar to the audience—which would have bogged the movie down had they all needed to be newly introduced. Marvel Studios even managed to bring Spider-Man into the Marvel Cinematic Universe (MCU), something fans once thought an impossibility given the film rights to the web-slinger reside with Sony Pictures Entertainment.

With Phase Three, Marvel Studios hit their stride. Not only does it have more films than the previous two phases, it also has more diversity, both in front of and behind the camera. The fact that the MCU has lasted this long is a testament to Marvel's focus on good storytelling, willingness to hire talented filmmakers irrespective of their experience, and careful cultivation of their characters. And to top it all off, audiences finally got to see Thanos take centre stage after being teased so many times. As the last block of films in what would be termed The Infinity Saga, Phase Three did not disappoint.

This book has been designed as a guide to Phase Three of the Marvel Cinematic Universe. You can read this book from beginning to end or simply dive into the chapters on your favourite movies. This book assumes you've seen the films before. There will be spoilers. For each movie, you'll find some information on its development and production (all monetary figures are in USD unless otherwise stated). Other sections include:

Excelsior!
A description of Stan Lee's cameo in the film.

Mid/Post-Credits Scene
A description of one or more of the film's stingers, should it have any.

Marvellous Miscellanea
Various interesting facts relating to the film.

From Panels to the Screen

Detailing homages, inspiration or any coincidental links made by the films to the comics. Generally, these are references to Marvel comics, although there is the occasional nod to material from other publishers. I'll also note how the films have influenced the comic books in turn.

For those that do not read comic books, the Marvel Multiverse is comprised of many universes or realities. These are also known as continuities and I will sometimes refer to a specific one. The continuity that most of Marvel's comics takes place in is known as the mainstream Marvel Universe, which has been designated Earth-616. Another notable universe is the Ultimate Universe (Earth-1610). Established in 2000, the many series taking place in this reality are modern interpretations of classic Marvel stories and characters. The Marvel Cinematic Universe—which is considered its own continuity—also goes by Earth-199999.

MCU Easter Eggs

Connections between the various Marvel Cinematic Universe entries.

Chopped, Changed, and Lengthened

Deleted, alternate, and extended scenes that aren't in the theatrical release, with an explanation as to why they were excised from the film wherever possible.

Location, Location

The various places used for shooting the film, with addresses for hopeful tourists. I will leave in-film locations or events in bold. Note that any entry costs are not listed, and some locations are not open to the public (e.g. a military base) or are private residences. (Take care not to disturb the owners!)

Although many areas are explored in this book, it is but a small fraction of the amount one can learn about the MCU. I encourage you to pick up the official *The Art of* books that Marvel releases for each film and to read industry-specific publications (e.g. *American Cinematographer*) covering areas you find of interest to expand your knowledge.

Marvel fans, assemble!

Andy Thai

PHASE THREE

PHASE THREE

CAPTAIN AMERICA: CIVIL WAR

Directors: Anthony and Joe Russo
Screenplay: Christopher Markus & Stephen McFeely

Producer: Kevin Feige
Executive Producers: Louis D'Esposito, Victoria Alonso, Patricia Whitcher, Nate Moore, and Stan Lee
Co-Producers: Mitch Bell, Christoph Fisser, Henning Molfenter, and Charlie Woebcken
Associate Producers: Lars P Winther, Trinh Tran, and Ari Costa

Cinematography: Trent Opaloch
Production Design: Owen Paterson
Editing: Jeffrey Ford and Matthew Schmidt
Music: Henry Jackman
Costume Design: Judianna Makovsky
Visual Effects Supervisor: Dan Deleeuw
Casting: Sarah Halley Finn

Production Company: Marvel Studios
Distribution Company: Walt Disney Studios Motion Pictures

US Release Date: 6 May 2016
Running Time: 147 minutes
Budget: $250 million
Box Office: $1,153,561,649

Based on the Marvel Comics by Joe Simon and Jack Kirby

Cast: Chris Evans (*Steve Rogers/Captain America*), Robert Downey Jr (*Tony Stark/Iron Man*), Scarlett Johansson (*Natasha Romanoff/Black Widow*), Sebastian Stan (*Bucky Barnes/Winter Soldier*), Anthony Mackie (*Sam Wilson/Falcon*), Don Cheadle (*Lieutenant James Rhodes/War Machine*), Jeremy Renner (*Clint Barton/Hawkeye*), Chadwick Boseman (*T'Challa/Black Panther*), Paul Bettany (*Vision*), Elizabeth Olsen (*Wanda Maximoff/Scarlet Witch*), Paul Rudd (*Scott Lang/Ant-Man*), Emily VanCamp (*Sharon Carter/Agent 13*), Tom Holland (*Peter Parker/Spider-Man*), Daniel Brühl (*Zemo*), Frank Grillo (*Brock Rumlow/Crossbones*), William Hurt (*Secretary of State Thaddeus Ross*), Martin Freeman (*Everett K Ross*), Marisa Tomei (*May Parker*), John Kani (*King T'Chaka*), John Slattery (*Howard Stark*), Hope Davis (*Maria Stark*), Alfre Woodard (*Miriam*), Ann Russo (*Voice of Zemo's Wife*), Gene Farber (*Karpov*), Florence Kasumba (*Security Chief*), Jim Rash (*MIT Liaison*), Sophia Russo (*Teenage Girl*), Gozie Agbo (*Dr Broussard*), Stan Lee (*FedEx Driver*), Kerry Condon (*FRIDAY*)

After the Avengers are involved in an incident that results in civilian casualties, a system to hold the super team accountable is implemented, one that also decides when the team deploys. This causes a rift in the team, with some siding with Tony Stark who supports oversight, and others siding with Steve Rogers who believes the team should operate without government interference.

Marvel Studios' complete Phase Three slate was announced on 28 October 2014 at the El Capitan Theatre in Los Angeles. During the presentation, it was revealed that the third *Captain America* film would be *Captain America: Serpent Society*—that is, until the true title was announced: *Captain America: Civil War*. Anthony and Joe Russo returned to direct what would be the third *Captain America* instalment, the pair envisioning the film as a psychological thriller and citing *Seven* (1995) and *Fargo* (1996) as influences.

Adapting this fan-favourite storyline—which saw Captain America pitted against Iron Man over the registration of superheroes—wouldn't have been the same had Robert Downey Jr decided not to sign on. It's alleged that Tony Stark initially had a small role, with Downey insisting his screen time be beefed up. This would have meant a higher pay for the actor, which the then-Marvel Entertainment CEO Isaac "Ike" Perlmutter was against. And while Perlmutter had the screenwriters omit the character because of this, Marvel Studios president Kevin Feige continued negotiations with Downey's representatives and they eventually reached a deal.

Civil War also saw T'Challa/Black Panther make his cinematic debut with Chadwick Boseman cast in the part. The character was included because the filmmakers decided that a third point of view was required, one not linked to Tony or Steve's agendas. Boseman didn't have to audition; the actor signed a five-picture deal after several discussions with Marvel. As part of the role, Boseman devised a Wakandan accent and learnt Xhosa, taught to him by John Kani who played T'Chaka, T'Challa's father.

The role of Zemo—the mysterious antagonist of *Civil War*—went to Daniel Brühl. The Spanish-born, German-raised actor was attracted to the role as he saw the character as something more than just another clichéd villain. Many other characters from the Marvel Cinematic Universe would also be included. Black Widow, Falcon, Sharon Carter, and Bucky Barnes return, continuing their arcs from *Captain America: The Winter Solider* (2014). Rhodey and Vision side with Tony in supporting the Sokovia Accords, while we see Hawkeye, Wanda Maximoff, and Ant-Man allying themselves with Steve, who's against it. We also see the return of Thaddeus Ross, who made his last appearance in 2008's *The Incredible Hulk*. With such a large cast—the film was dubbed *Avengers 2.5* by some fans—writers Christopher Markus and Stephen McFeely were mindful of keeping the focus on Chris Evans' Captain America. Unlike the previous two *Captain America* films, there wasn't a clear enemy this time, with Steve fighting his friends over a moral quandary with no easy solution.

Principal photography commenced on 27 April 2015 at Pinewood Atlanta Studios. Production moved to Germany for the last four weeks of shooting and wrapped in Leipzig on 21 August the same year.

One of the film's signature scenes is the fight at Leipzig/Halle Airport, which serves as the climax of the second act. Referred to by the Russos as the "splash panel" (an image that usually takes up two pages in a comic book), it ended up becoming one of the film's biggest sequences. Though most of the film was shot with Arri Alexa XT Plus digital cameras, the sixteen-minute action scene was captured using the IMAX-customised Arri Alexa 65. *Civil War* was the first production to use the new technology.

Logistically, shooting the scene was very complex. Background plates of the actual airport were shot, with some of the action captured on location with the cast members that were present in Germany. The vast remainder of the scene was shot against green screen in Atlanta with a CG environment. Initially, it was planned that only CG enhancements were required for the Black Panther suit, such as the removal of wrinkles and addition of the lenses and claws. However, the design of the costume underwent several changes during post-production resulting in much of the practical suit being replaced with a digital one.

Another character that played a crucial role in the comic book story was Spider-Man. Marvel Studios and Sony Pictures Entertainment were both involved with the search for the new Peter Parker, owing to the deal they had made to bring Spidey into the MCU. (For more details see the *Spider-Man: Homecoming* chapter.) A teenage actor was sought, and by the end of May 2015 there were six final contenders: Asa Butterfield, Tom Holland, Judah Lewis, Matthew Lintz, Charlie Plummer, and Charlie Rowe. After screen tests with Robert Downey Jr and Chris Evans, nineteen-year-old Holland won the role. It didn't hurt that his *In the Heart of the Sea* (2016) co-star Chris Hemsworth also put in a good word for him. The English actor found out he got the part by going online and stumbling across a post on Marvel's Instagram page telling people to visit marvel.com to discover who'll be playing the web-swinger. Holland signed on for six films, three being solo Spider-Man outings.

Though Holland wore a physical Spider-Man costume on set (this one had a raised webbing pattern and a differently shaped spider for the chest emblem), it was redesigned during post-production. In fact, Spider-Man also wound up being a completely digital creation in the final film. To reflect the character's youth and inexperience, his movements were animated off-balance at times and the filmmakers consciously refrained from using his iconic poses from the comic books.

As a diversion to help Captain America and Bucky get away, Ant-Man transforms into Giant-Man. The Russo brothers fought to include this, reasoning that it was a visually impressive and unexpected way to turn the tide of the fight. Had they not been able to include the character, they alternatively planned for Wanda Maximoff to light up a fuel line and cause a large explosion. While Scott Lang's previous Ant-Man suit was designed to look as though it was created during the '60s, the character was given a more modern-looking costume this time around, the helmet changing the most. Giant-Man's movements were kept slow to communicate his large size, with Paul Rudd's performance used as a reference for the visual effects artists.

The world premiere for *Captain America: Civil War* was held at the Dolby Theater in Hollywood on 12 April 2016. The film was a critical success and box office hit, with critics praising the thought-provoking story and action set pieces. *Civil War* became the highest grossing film of 2016 worldwide.

Audiences came for the spectacle but were left grappling some of the big questions the film posed, with the contrast of Tony's utilitarian approach against Steve Rogers' more principled view showing how the answers aren't always as clear-cut as we'd like to think.

Excelsior!
Stan Lee appears as a FedEx delivery man who has a package for "Tony Stank."

Mid-Credits Scene
Steve and Bucky are in Wakanda, where Bucky voluntarily goes back into cryosleep until his Winter Soldier programming can be cured.

Post-Credits Scene
Peter Parker is back at home nursing his injuries, telling Aunt May that he got into a fight with a guy named Steve from Brooklyn. After she leaves his room, he looks at the Spider-Signal that's projecting from his web shooter.

Marvellous Miscellanea
- Had Robert Downey Jr decided not to return as Tony Stark in *Civil War*, it was suggested that the "Madbomb" storyline (*Captain America* #193-200, 1976) could be adapted instead. The film would have seen Zemo set off the Madbomb—a device that causes those in range of the explosion to become violent. This would have challenged Captain America physically and morally, with the character needing to fight civilians as well as his fellow heroes.
- *Sputnik* was the working title used for the film. In the comics, "Sputnik" is a code word used to shut down the Winter Soldier.
- Damion Poitier, who portrayed Thanos in *The Avengers* (2012), appears in *Civil War* as the mercenary who threatens to drop the biological weapon vial.
- The last thing Robert Downey Jr shot for the film was the B.A.R.F. hologram sequence, which necessitated the actor to shave off his beard.
- The MIT Liaison is played by Jim Rash, who appeared on *Community* (2009-15) as Craig Pelton, the dean of Greendale Community College.
- Before her role in *Civil War* was revealed, fans speculated that Alfre Woodard was going to appear as Mariah Dillard, the character she plays

in the Marvel-Netflix television series *Luke Cage* (2016-18). It would eventually be confirmed that her character was named Miriam, meaning the actress would be portraying two different characters in the MCU. This could be chalked up to a lack of communication between Marvel Studios and Marvel Television.
- The letter 'D' and the number twenty-three can be spotted adorning the Winter Soldier containment chamber, a reference to D23, the official Disney fan club.
- Ann Russo, the wife of Anthony Russo, provided the voice of Zemo's wife.
- Several stunt doubles make cameo appearances during the flashback in which we see Hydra's Super-Soldier experiments. Heidi Moneymaker, who doubles for Scarlett Johansson, is the closest female receiving the Super-Soldier serum intravenously. Jackson Spidell, who doubles for Chris Evans in the film, plays the Winter Soldier named Josef. Aaron Toney, who doubles for Anthony Mackie, also appears as a Winter Soldier.
- The moment when Tony Stark tells Peter Parker to move his leg so he can sit on the bed was improvised. Tom Holland had forgotten the blocking of the scene and so Robert Downey Jr reminded him whilst staying in character.
- The Bluth family's stair car from *Arrested Development* (2003-19) can be spotted in the background during the airport fight. The Russos co-directed the series' pilot episode and have directed several episodes individually as well.
- While Joe Russo portrays Dr Broussard in the film, an on-set production assistant portrayed the character's corpse in the bathtub when the hotel housekeeper finds him. This was done so the director could be at the monitor and film the scene. The character's name appears to be a nod to frequent MCU producer Stephen Broussard.
- An Inhumans film was announced as part of Marvel's Phase Three slate, with a planned release date of 2 November 2018. It wouldn't eventuate, with a television show being made instead.

From Panels to the Screen
The Serpent Society, used in the fake title for *Captain America: Civil War* during Marvel's Phase Three announcement, is a criminal organisation comprised

of snake-themed villains such as Sidewinder, King Cobra, and Anaconda.

The film is based on the "Civil War" crossover event, the core story being told across *Civil War* #1-7 (2006-07). The villain, Nitro, uses his self-exploding powers in an attempt to avoid capture by the New Warriors (a group consisting of young superheroes) and ends up killing hundreds of civilians, including children. This leads to the introduction of the Superhuman Registration Act, which requires those with powers to register their true identity so they can be held accountable for any misdeeds and collateral damage that may occur through their work. Those siding with Iron Man on the pro-registration side include Mister Fantastic, Hank Pym (actually the Skrull Criti Noll in disguise), She-Hulk, Carol Danvers/Ms Marvel, and Sentry. Captain America leads the heroes that are anti-registration, with Falcon, Kate Bishop/Hawkeye, Daredevil (Danny Rand posing as the vigilante), Black Panther, Jonas/Vision, Hercules, and Goliath amongst his team. Spider-Man initially supports Iron Man, but later switches sides and joins the anti-registration team. In *Captain America: Civil War*, the two sides fight over the formation of a governing body that decides when the Avengers should be deployed. Captain America, Bucky Barnes, Falcon, Hawkeye, Wanda Maximoff, Sharon Carter, and Ant-Man oppose this action, with Iron Man, War Machine, Black Widow, Black Panther, and Vision supporting the decision.

In the comics, Sam Wilson owns a pet falcon, Redwing, with which he has a telepathic link. This was reimagined as a drone for his cinematic outing. We see Brock Rumlow as Crossbones in the film; his skull mask and the white 'X' on his outfit is similar to the costume he wears in the source material. In the comics, Helmut Zemo is the son of Nazi scientist Heinrich Zemo, both of whom have used the Baron Zemo moniker. A supervillain following in his father's footsteps, Helmut Zemo is usually clad in a purple hood that hides his scarred visage.

In the film, Colonel Vasily Karpov ran the Siberian Winter Soldier training facility and was a member of Hydra and the Russian Armed Forces. His comic book counterpart was a Russian officer and is similarly tied to Bucky Barnes, being instrumental in turning him into the Winter Solider. To prove that the Winter Soldier programming is not currently active for him, Bucky reveals that Steve's mother was named Sarah, a fact that's also true of her counterpart in the source material.

The character of Miriam is a reference to Miriam Sharpe, a mother whose son, Damien (changed to Charlie Spencer in the MCU), was killed by Nitro.

Both incarnations of the character are responsible for Tony Stark changing his view on having superheroes kept in check. During Peggy Carter's funeral—an event that has been depicted in the comics, occurring in *Captain America* #1 (2011)—Sharon Carter recites her aunt's "No, you move" speech. In *The Amazing Spider-Man* #537 (2007), it is Captain America who delivers the iconic message to Spider-Man, reassuring him that going against the Superhuman Registration Act was the right thing to do.

In the source material, T'Challa is the ruler of Wakanda and is the current holder of the Black Panther title. An accomplished tracker and strategist, T'Challa's physical capabilities and senses have all been enhanced due to a heart-shaped herb he ingested. Only those of royal blood can safely consume the rare herb. In both media, his father, T'Chaka, was king before him. In the comics, it was Ulysses Klaw who killed T'Chaka, whereas in the film, he's killed in an explosion set by Helmut Zemo.

The comic book incarnation of Everett Ross is a US State Department employee who was tasked with escorting T'Challa during his time in New York City. Since then, Ross has become an expert on Wakanda and has aided T'Challa on several occasions. His cinematic counterpart is aligned with the Joint Counter Terrorist Centre. T'Challa's bodyguards are known as the Dora Milaje. In the comics, the Dora Milaje are an all-female group tasked with protecting the Black Panther and the royal family. Originally, each member served as a potential bride for the king, though this had evolved over Wakandan history to become a symbolic gesture.

Both the comic book and MCU incarnations of Peter Parker/Spider-Man possess enhanced strength, fast reflexes, the ability to crawl on surfaces, and a danger-warning spider-sense. We also see the character use his trademark web shooters, which he uses to swing about and incapacitate enemies. True to the source material, Holland's Spidey lives with his aunt, May Parker, and hails from Queens, New York. The cinematic version of Peter mentions to Tony that he hasn't gotten his driver's licence, a trait he shares with his comic book counterpart (living in New York, he doesn't really need one to get around Manhattan). The moving lenses on Spider-Man's costume could be a nod to how artists would change the size of the lenses when drawing Spidey, as a way of expressing his emotions. The light we see Peter play with in the post-credits scene is known as the Spider-Signal. Traditionally located on his belt, Spidey uses it to announce his presence to criminals in the comics.

The Mark 46 Iron Man armour, with its multiple arc reactors, resembles the Bleeding Edge armour from the comics. Hawkeye firing an arrow with a shrunken Scott Lang/Ant-Man riding on it is a moment taken from *The Avengers* #223 (1982), the iconic move also adorning the issue's cover. The film has a shrunken Ant-Man entering Iron Man's armour in an attempt to disable it. In *Iron Man* #133 (1980), a similar incident occurs, though in this case Ant-Man is trying to fix the armour. Notably in both media, the character has to contend with the Iron Man armour's fire suppression system. During the film's airport battle, we see Scott Lang use Pym Particles to grow in size, becoming Giant-Man. Several characters in the source material have used this identity, including Hank Pym, Bill Foster, and Raz Malhotra.

In both media, the Raft is a prison designed to contain enhanced individuals. It made its first appearance in *Alias* #26 (2003). Captain America uses his shield to block a stream of blasts from Iron Man at the Siberian Hydra facility, which is a recreation of the cover to *Civil War* #7 (2007). Later in the fight, Iron Man uses his suit to analyse and predict Cap's fighting style, something his comic book counterpart does in *Civil War* #3 (2006).

MCU Easter Eggs

Steve's sketch of a monkey riding a unicycle from *Captain America: The First Avenger* (2011) can be seen in his office. He also says, "I could do this all day," to Tony towards the end of their fight (which he uttered in *The First Avenger*). Photographs of a young Pietro Maximoff can be seen in Wanda's room. The Chitauri invasion of New York, the Helicarriers falling out of the sky over Washington DC, and the incident in Sokovia are all referenced in the film. Ultron heads can be seen painted on War Machine's armour, indicating the number of Ultron Sentries he destroyed in *Avengers: Age of Ultron* (2015). And while "homecoming" was used as one of the trigger words to activate the Winter Soldier, it was a coincidence that it would also be used in the title of Spider-Man's first solo MCU film, with the writers of *Civil War* having chosen the words they did as they liked how they sounded in Russian.

Chopped, Changed, and Lengthened

- At one point, the Hulk and the Wasp were to have made appearances in *Captain America: Civil War*. The Hulk was present in versions of the script, but Marvel Studios wanted to save the reveal of where the character went post-*Age of Ultron* for another project. The Wasp was also included in early drafts but omitted as it was decided that Hope van

Dyne donning the costume needed to be established first before being included in an ensemble.
- Before Marvel's deal with Sony to bring Spider-Man into the MCU, an early draft of the script saw Tony Stark travel to San Francisco to recruit Scott Lang to fight on his side.
- In Russia, the text and Russian flag on the sleeves of the Hydra soldiers were digitally removed. The change was requested by Disney Russia, the company not wanting Russia to be associated with Hydra and, in turn, villainy.
- Originally, Zemo was to have obtained the red Winter Soldier book from a black market auction, gassing everyone at the event before stealing it. It didn't end up being used as it didn't have any link to the flashback that opens the film.
- When Natasha Romanoff asks Tony where his potential recruit could be found, the scene was shot with Tony responding with "Queens." It was edited so the word would appear over the establishing shot of the borough instead.
- Sharon Carter's speech at Peggy's funeral was originally longer. She ended by recounting the time she asked what her aunt's proudest achievement was; Peggy had responded that the information was classified. This is followed by an extended conversation Natasha has with Steve after the service, with Natasha mentioning how she went back to Russia to find her parents and leaving flowers at their graves.
- After Peggy's funeral, Steve and Sharon meet up for drinks. They discuss whether or not Peggy knew Sharon was tasked with spying on Steve, how Sharon is now based in Berlin working for the Joint Terrorism Task Force (a conversation that's moved to Sharon's hotel in the film, taking place as the pair wait for an elevator), as well as the impending Sokovia Accords.
- Zemo listens to a message on his phone from his wife. Hanging up, he sees Dr Broussard get off the train and goes to greet him.
- Natasha talks to T'Challa at the headquarters of the Joint Counter Terrorist Centre, attempting to perform a psychological evaluation on him. Everett Ross then walks into the room, informing T'Challa that Bucky will be extradited to Wakanda.
- During the airport battle, War Machine shoots at Captain America who then falls. Bucky runs towards Captain America, picking up his shield

and throwing it at War Machine. Falcon flies by, catching the shield and tossing it back to Captain America. Bucky remarks that he needs to get himself a shield before they run off.

Location, Location

Captain America: Civil War takes place in many international locations and, fittingly, scenes were shot in many different countries, though usually as a stand-in for another locale. The film begins in **Siberia**, with CG-altered footage of Iceland used for the establishing shots.

After the flashback, we find our heroes in Lagos, Nigeria. When **Falcon looks out at the city**, it's actually Puerto Rico he's surveying, specifically San Juan's Milla de Oro. The building he's standing on is the World Plaza Building (268 Avenida Luis Muñoz Rivera, San Juan). Falcon has **Redwing follow and inspect a garbage truck**, the vehicle travelling down Avenida Borinquen between Calle San Antonio and Calle Argentina. The Boisfeuillet Jones Atlanta Civic Center (395 Piedmont Avenue NE, Atlanta, Georgia) stood in for the **Institute for Infectious Diseases** in Lagos. The theatre was also used for the **MIT auditorium** where Tony Stark announces the September Foundation Grant. The Avengers then follow Crossbones to a **Lagosian market**, which was created in the Gulch area in Downtown Atlanta (specifically in the area behind the Norfolk Southern Building at 125 Spring Street SW). When Crossbones activates his bomb vest, Scarlet Witch attempts to contain and redirect the explosion but accidentally destroys part of a building, which is the nearby Richard B Russell Federal Building and United States Courthouse (75 Ted Turner Drive SW, Atlanta).

The Porsche Experience Center in Atlanta (One Porsche Drive) is used as a building at the **New Avengers facility**. Note that the aerial shot of the headquarters shows both the Porsche Experience Center and the Sainsbury Centre for Visual Arts in England (which was used in *Avengers: Age of Ultron*). The two buildings were added to a plate

Atlanta, Georgia

of an area next to the Hudson River in the New York town of Esopus. Though the film indicates **Peggy Carter's funeral** is held in London, the scene was filmed at Peachtree Christian Church (1580 Peachtree Street NW, Atlanta). For the **hotel** Sharon Carter and Steve Rogers visit, the filmmakers used the LINE LA (3515 Wilshire Boulevard, Los Angeles, California).

The establishing shot of Vienna depicts the **Vienna International Centre** (Wagramer Straße 5), which houses several of the United Nations' organisations. The **United Nations conference** was filmed at the Sony Center (Potsdamer Straße 4) in Berlin, Germany. After the bomb blast, the survivors are gathered at the nearby Henriette-Herz-Park. The **restaurant** where Sharon gives Steve some intel on Bucky's whereabouts was shot at Lutter and Wegner (Bellevuestraße 1, Berlin). While the film has us believe that the **market** Bucky visits is in Bucharest, Romania, we're actually still in Germany, the stalls having been set up in front of the buildings on both sides of Leipziger Straße in Berlin (around where it meets Jerusalemer Straße). Jumping from his apartment, Bucky lands on the **adjacent building** where he encounters the Black Panther. While the jump was filmed against green screen, the building he lands on is real, being the Internationales Congress Centrum Berlin. The 320-metre-long convention centre can be found in the Westend locality of the borough Charlottenburg-Wilmersdorf. The chase progresses to a **tunnel**, the filmmakers having shot the sequence at Berlin's Messedamm Underpass. The location, with its distinctive orange pillars, can also be seen in *The Bourne Supremacy* (2004), *Hanna* (2011), and *The Hunger Games: Mockingjay – Part 2* (2015).

A shot of the **Victory Column** (located at the *Großer Stern* roundabout) is used to establish Berlin before we see the motorcade driving down Kapelle-Ufer then crossing the **Spree River** via the **Crown Prince Bridge** (or *Kronprinzenbrücke* in German). They soon arrive at the **Joint Counter Terrorist Centre Buildings**, which digitally replaces the Paul-Löbe-Haus (Konrad-Adenauer-Straße 1, Berlin) and Marie-Elisabeth-Lüders-Haus (Adele-Schreiber-Krieger-Straße 1, Berlin). Despite having shot footage in the area, the filmmakers were not allowed to feature the parliamentary buildings on-screen. The interior area, where Bucky fights Tony, Sharon, Natasha, and T'Challa, was filmed all

The Victory Column

the way back in Georgia at the James M Baker University Center, a part of Clayton State University (2000 Clayton State Boulevard, Morrow, Georgia). The **transformer station** that Zemo has an EMP device delivered to isn't in Berlin, but rather at the southern end of Cherokee Avenue SE in Atlanta.

The **parking garage** where Scott Lang meets Steve is the AT&T car park, located at 759 West Peachtree Street NW, Atlanta. This is then followed by the fight at **Leipzig/Halle Airport** in Schkeuditz between Iron Man's and Captain America's sides. While mostly filmed against green screen at Pinewood Atlanta Studios (461 Sandy Creek Road, Fayetteville, Georgia)—which has since changed its name to Trilith Studios—the filmmakers did shoot background plates at the real location.

DOCTOR STRANGE

Director: Scott Derrickson
Screenplay: Jon Spaihts and Scott Derrickson & C Robert Cargill

Producer: Kevin Feige
Executive Producers: Louis D'Esposito, Victoria Alonso, Stephen Broussard, Charles Newirth, and Stan Lee
Co-Producer: David J Grant

Cinematography: Ben Davis
Production Design: Charles Wood
Editing: Wyatt Smith and Sabrina Plisco
Music: Michael Giacchino
Costume Design: Alexandra Byrne
Visual Effects Supervisor: Stephane Ceretti
Casting: Sarah Halley Finn

Production Company: Marvel Studios
Distribution Company: Walt Disney Studios Motion Pictures

US Release Date: 4 November 2016
Running Time: 115 minutes
Budget: $165 million
Box Office: $677,796,076

Based on the Marvel Comics by Stan Lee and Steve Ditko

Cast: Benedict Cumberbatch (*Dr Stephen Strange/Doctor Strange*), Chiwetel Ejiofor (*Mordo*), Rachel McAdams (*Dr Christine Palmer*), Benedict Wong (*Wong*), Mads Mikkelsen (*Kaecilius*), Tilda Swinton (*The Ancient One*), Michael Stuhlbarg (*Dr Nicodemus West*), Benjamin Bratt (*Jonathan Pangborn*), Scott Adkins (*Lucian*), Zara Phythian (*Brunette Zealot*), Alaa Safi (*Tall Zealot*), Katrina Durden (*Blonde Zealot*), Topo Wresniwiro (*Hamir*), Umit Ulgen (*Sol Rama*), Linda Duan (*Tina Minoru*), Mark Anthony Brighton (*Daniel Drumm*), Kobna Holdbrook-Smith (*Physical Therapist*), Stan Lee (*Bus Passenger*), Pat Kiernan (*Himself*), Chris Hemsworth (*Thor*)

Renowned neurosurgeon Doctor Stephen Strange loses the use of his hands in a car accident. After conventional medicine fails to heal his injuries, Stephen travels to Kamar-Taj as a last resort, a journey that leads him to discover the mystic arts.

Doctor Strange is certainly one of Marvel's more unique heroes. The supernatural and different dimensions are hallmarks of the character, and presenting all of this to a mainstream movie audience would require a cast and crew with the right vision. During the early '90s, Wes Craven signed on to write and direct when the project was at Savoy Pictures. Nothing eventuated, with Columbia Pictures having a go, hiring Jeff Welch to have a crack at the script. By 2001, Dimension Films held the rights, the studio wanting David S Goyer as director in addition to his writing duties (he had previously written a version for Columbia). Marvel Studios eventually reacquired the rights and revealed that a Doctor Strange movie would be part of their Phase Three lineup.

In June 2014, it was announced that Scott Derrickson would occupy the director's chair. Derrickson is known for his work on horror films having written and directed *The Exorcism of Emily Rose* (2005), *Sinister* (2012), and *Deliver Us From Evil* (2014). The director had eight meetings with Marvel Studios before landing the gig. Derrickson scripted the astral plane fight with writer C Robert Cargill and had the sequence storyboarded, an animatic created, as well as spending his own money to get concept art made, all in an effort to demonstrate his vision for the film and show the passion he had for his favourite comic book character.

Casting then occurred over the following months. Ethan Hawke, Jared Leto, and Oscar Isaac were reportedly considered for Stephen Strange. Derrickson met with Joaquin Phoenix, but it would be Benedict Cumberbatch—a well-known figure amongst pop culture fans, having portrayed Sherlock Holmes, Khan Noonien Singh, and Smaug—who ended up signing on to play the sorcerer. Derrickson flew to London to meet with the actor and talk about the movie even though there wasn't a script. Despite being the director's preferred choice for the role, at the time Cumberbatch couldn't commit due to his role as the titular character in the Barbican Theatre's production of *Hamlet*. After meeting with other actors for the part, it was eventually decided that the film's production schedule would be modified and the release date pushed back to enable Cumberbatch to come on board.

Rachel McAdams was cast as fellow surgeon Christine Palmer. Originally, the character was written as Stephen's love interest, but Derrickson decided to change that, making them ex-partners instead. To prepare, both McAdams and Cumberbatch researched neurosurgery and consulted with an actual neurosurgeon on set, learning about the procedures and instruments they use.

One of Doctor Strange's best-known foes from the comics, Karl Mordo, was changed for the film, starting off as a mentor to Stephen before a rift occurs between the two characters. Chiwetel Ejiofor scored the part, the actor looking to the comics to gain an understanding of the character.

Probably the hardest role to cast was that of the Ancient One, but not due to a lack of talent. In the comics, the Ancient One is an elderly Asian male, but wanting to avoid the Fu Manchu stereotype, Derrickson decided to cast a female in the part. This, though, could have also led to negative connotations, with an elderly Asian female possibly evoking the Dragon Lady stereotype. Eventually, British actress Tilda Swinton was cast, but this proved controversial too, the decision labelled another instance of whitewashing. Stressing that there was no malintent behind the hiring of Swinton, Derrickson did acknowledge that while the decision wasn't the best, it was certainly better than perpetuating a negative stereotype.

If casting the Ancient One was considered a backwards step in the representations of Asians in Hollywood, then the casting of Wong was a conscious effort to fix this. Stephen's servant in the comics, Wong proved to be another tricky character to include, and was almost excluded as a result. But with the Ancient One no longer being Asian, Derrickson decided to include the character after all. To remedy the character's anachronistic role, Wong was made Kamar-Taj's librarian and mentor to Stephen. Benedict Wong would be cast, having heard of the project from Ejiofor, the pair having previously worked together on *Dirty Pretty Things* (2002) and *The Martian* (2015). As for the film's antagonist, Danish actor Mads Mikkelsen would be cast as Kaecilius. Mikkelsen relished the idea of playing a character with a complex viewpoint and martial arts abilities.

Principal photography commenced in November 2015, beginning with a four-day shoot in Nepal and finishing on 3 April 2016 in New York City. While locations were scouted in Nepal, the Gorkha earthquake destroyed many of them when it struck the country on 25 April 2015. Nonetheless, Derrickson went on to film around the Kathmandu Valley in an effort to bring more tourism back to the area.

Given the film's focus on magic and exploration of different dimensions, visual effects were heavily relied upon to bring scenes to life. This was made tougher given the movie's short post-production period, precipitated by the altered schedule to accommodate Cumberbatch's involvement, resulting in more VFX vendors being hired than usual.

When Stephen initially meets the Ancient One, she shatters his scepticism in the mystic arts by sending him on what the filmmakers called the Magical Mystery Tour. The trippy sequence sees the doctor whizzing through various dimensions, each one trippier and more absurd than the last. Various references were used to design the sequence, such as fractal art, electron microscope photography, and Mandelbulbs. Though Cumberbatch was attached to a gimbal rig and filmed against green screen, a digital double was used for many shots, given the different rules of gravity in the dimensions he visits. Conceived to be approximately seven minutes in length, the sequence was trimmed down to roughly two minutes owing to the film's pace.

For sequences set in the Mirror Dimension—which sees the landscape around the characters twist and become kaleidoscopic—the filmmakers pulled inspiration from the mobile game *Monument Valley*, German expressionistic art, mandalas, the works of M C Escher and Salvador Dalí, and, of course, *Inception* (2010). Industrial Light & Magic were tasked with working on the chase through Manhattan. Actors were filmed on green screen sets, with wires, treadmills, motion bases, and gimbals used to simulate the effects the ever-changing landscape had on the characters. Plate shoots and lidar scans of New York were conducted and information was obtained from NYC Open Data, which allowed the company to create the city digitally. Getting the textures of real-world objects was paramount to grounding the shots in reality, despite the surreal and absurd ways they would behave.

The film's climax sees Doctor Strange entering the Dark Dimension to confront Dormammu directly. The idea was to subvert the ending of previous Marvel films—where the villain destroys a city—and have a city reconstructed instead. Steve Ditko's renderings of Dormammu's hostile realm from the comics were used as the basis for its design on-screen. The director was also inspired by a Doctor Strange black light poster from 1971 that he owns, resulting in a psychedelic, neon-coloured environment. The idea of Cumberbatch portraying Dormammu was put forth to Derrickson by the actor himself. The director allowed this, reasoning that the character doesn't have a human form and so mirrors Stephen. Cumberbatch provided the facial mocap for Dormammu. He also voiced the character and this was combined with that of another undisclosed British actor. As an alternative option, Tony Todd also recorded lines for Dormammu, but these were ultimately not used.

After a red carpet event in Hong Kong on 13 October 2016, *Doctor Strange* had its world premiere at Grauman's Chinese Theatre in Hollywood on 20 October 2016. Audiences praised the film's mind-bending visuals but were more critical with Stephen's character arc, observing how similar it was to other MCU origin stories. Magic and the manipulation of time were important elements in Marvel Studios' latest entry, but fans would soon discover that they were integral elements to the MCU as well.

Excelsior!

During the fight with Kaecilius in the streets of New York, Doctor Strange and Mordo slam into a bus in which Stan Lee is riding, the former Marvel comic book writer reading *The Doors of Perception* by Aldous Huxley. The cameo was one of four Stan Lee shot that day in Atlanta, three of which (including this one) were filmed by James Gunn. Other options shot for *Doctor Strange* include Lee laughing and saying, "I'm laughing for no reason! I'm totally crazy!," Lee reading a book and asking the person next to him, "Do you know what 'excelsior' means?," and Lee reading a *Garfield* book and exclaiming, "He *hates* Mondays, but he *loves* lasagna!"

Mid-Credits Scene

In a scene taken from *Thor: Ragnarok*, Thor visits Doctor Strange at the New York Sanctum Sanctorum, asking for his help in locating Odin. Strange agrees to help after hearing that Thor and Loki will return to Asgard once Odin is found. Shot in London and directed by Taika Waititi, the scene was filmed several months before principal photography began on *Ragnarok*.

Post-Credits Scene
Mordo tracks down Jonathan Pangborn and takes away the mystical energy that enables him to walk, decreeing that there are too many sorcerers in the world.

Marvellous Miscellanea
- *Checkmate* was the working title used for the film during principal photography.
- At one point, Derrickson considered using Nightmare as the antagonist of the film. He decided against it when Kevin Feige pointed out the difficulty in having to explain the Dimension of Dreams in a film that already introduces a lot of different concepts.
- A new Marvel Studios logo can be seen at the beginning of *Doctor Strange*. Created by design company Perception, the new iteration incorporates script extracts, concept art, clips from the MCU films, as well as the iconic flipping Marvel logo, encapsulating how the MCU is brought to life. The sequence is accompanied by a fanfare composed by Michael Giacchino.
- While a majority of the film was shot using digital cameras, daylight exterior scenes filmed in Nepal were captured using celluloid film, as both Derrickson and cinematographer Ben Davis prefer the way it looked.
- A lot of real medical equipment was used in the hospital scenes. Adding to the realism was the fact that some of the extras hired had actual medical experience.
- Stephen's car accident occurs on 2 February (as indicated on the watch he selects to wear to the Neurological Society dinner), which is Groundhog Day, foreshadowing the film's timeloop climax.
- Lamborghini provided the filmmakers with eight Huracán LP610-4s to shoot Stephen's car accident: two for scenes shot in New York and six for the portion shot in the UK.
- It took about an hour-and-a-half to get the bald cap applied on Tilda Swinton. Mads Mikkelsen, meanwhile, had to endure a two- to three-hour makeup process to get the cracked-skin look around his eyes.
- The colours of the clothes people wear at Kamar-Taj represent their rank. Novices wear grey, apprentices are dressed in red, disciples are clad in blue, while masters get to choose their own outfits.
- The filmmakers turned to Julian Daniels (also known as JayFunk)—a

martial artist and practitioner of the tutting dance style—to develop the arm movements and hand gestures the sorcerers use when conjuring magic.
- Conlanger David J Peterson once again contributes to the MCU, creating Nelvayu, the language spoken by Kaecilius and his Zealots.
- Various architectural styles were used as inspiration for the design of the New York Sanctum Sanctorum including Art Deco, Bauhaus, Neo-classical, and Regency. The distinctive oculus window has a diameter of fourteen feet (4.3 metres) and took approximately four months to design and create.
- Derrickson wanted to use "Are You Experienced?" by the Jimi Hendrix Experience or Pink Floyd's "Interstellar Overdrive" over the credits but both songs were cost-prohibitive. Whilst the latter can be heard in the film before Stephen's car accident, composer Michael Giacchino came up with the track "The Master of the Mystic End Credits" for the end credits instead.
- *Rick and Morty* (2013-) co-creator Dan Harmon was shown a cut of the film and asked to give his opinion on it. He even contributed some jokes for scenes done during additional photography, though according to Derrickson many weren't used in the final film.
- *Doctor Strange* was nominated for Best Visual Effects at the 89th Academy Awards. It lost out to *The Jungle Book* (2016).

From Panels to the Screen

The film largely follows Doctor Strange's origin story from *Strange Tales* #115 (1963). Stephen Strange was a talented neurosurgeon until one day he was involved in a car accident that damaged the nerves in his hands, rendering him unable to operate on people. Wanting to find a cure, he eventually makes his way to Tibet and there meets the Ancient One. The Ancient One refuses to help Stephen, but after the doctor is unable to warn the old sorcerer of an attack from Karl Mordo (a student of the Ancient One) because of a spell placed on him, Stephen becomes his pupil and is taught the mystical arts. Serving as the Sorcerer Supreme—Earth's magical protector—Doctor Strange draws power from various sources and is able to cast illusions, astrally project himself, teleport, and manipulate energy, amongst other abilities. His signature equipment includes the Cloak of Levitation (which enables him to fly) and the Eye of Agamotto (an amulet that can create portals, grant the user telepathy, and emits a light that weakens evil beings and uncovers illusions). In the comics, the Eye of Agamotto is its own artefact and does not contain the Time Gem.

While the film places the temple of Kamar-Taj in Nepal, in the comics it's the name of a village located in Tibet and also the location of the Ancient One's palace. In the comics, Yao/the Ancient One is male and of Tibetan descent, while the cinematic version is female and has a Celtic background (her real name is unrevealed). Both, as their title implies, are centuries old and are highly proficient in the mystic arts.

The cinematic incarnation of Mordo is a skilled sorcerer, as per the comic books. It must be noted that in the source material he's Transylvanian with Caucasian skin and holds the rank of baron. In the movie, Mordo tells Stephen that the wi-fi password is "shamballa," a reference to the Doctor Strange graphic novel *Into Shamballa* (1986). The film incarnation of Wong is a Master of the Mystic Arts and Kamar-Taj's librarian, a change from his comic book counterpart who works as a servant for Doctor Strange.

The comic book version of Kaecilius was a disciple of Mordo's who helped him in his quest to defeat Doctor Strange. He would later be banished to the Purple Dimension. In the comics, Dormammu was born in the Dimension of the Faltines. After killing their parent—Sinifer—Dormammu and his sister, Umar, were banished but came to reside in the Dark Dimension, home of the magic-wielding Mhuruuks. The siblings would go on to show Olnar, king of the Dark Dimension, how to conquer other dimensions. When Olnar tried to absorb the dimension of the Mindless Ones, the Mindless Ones killed him, with Dormammu subsequently becoming ruler. An entity comprised of energy, he possesses immense power and numerous abilities, such as size-shifting, teleportation, and telepathy. He's usually depicted with a head that's constantly on fire.

While a doctor in the film, the Christine Palmer of the comics is a nurse (one of several to be referred to as "Night Nurse") working at Metropolitan General Hospital. Stephen appearing in his astral form to Christine as she operates on him is taken from *Doctor Strange: The Oath* #1 (2006). Interestingly, the story features a Night Nurse, but it's Linda Carter not Christine.

In the source material, Dr Nicodemus West was the surgeon who operated on Stephen Strange's hands after his car accident. Feeling guilty about the failure of the surgery, he tracks Stephen down to Kamar-Taj. With Stephen having already left, however, the Ancient One proceeds to teach Nicodemus the mystical arts, though Nicodemus leaves before he can complete his training.

The film's one-handed sorcerer, Hamir, could be a reference to Hamir the Hermit, who was an attendant to the Ancient One and Wong's father in the source material. The previous Master of the New York Sanctum is Daniel Drumm, who in the comics was a practitioner of voodoo. His spirit was later bound to his brother, Jericho Drumm, who took on the role of Brother Voodoo after him. The Master of the Hong Kong Sanctum is Tina Minoru. Her comic book counterpart is a sorceress as well, though she is a member of the criminal organisation Pride. The object we see Tina wield in the film is the Staff of One. In the comics, it allows the user to cast any spell, but only responds to each incantation once.

In both media, Strange operates out of his Sanctum Sanctorum, located at 177A Bleecker Street in New York City's Greenwich Village. A single location in the comics, the film sees Sanctums added to Hong Kong and London. Numerous mystical artefacts are housed in the New York Sanctum, including the Brazier of Bom'Galiath (an object that allows the user to use a spell for an extended period of time), the Crimson Bands of Cyttorak (depicted as metal restraints in the film, the Bands are a mystical spell in the comics), and the Daggers of Daveroth (physical daggers in the film; again, a spell in the comics).

Other relics in the film are either lifted straight from the source material or have some links to it. The Book of Cagliostro, which Kaecilius rips pages out of, is a tome of mystical knowledge compiled by the sorcerer Cagliostro in the comics. Mordo teaches Stephen about the Staff of the Living Tribunal, Wand of Watoomb, and Vaulting Boots of Valtorr during a training session. The Staff of the Living Tribunal is a reference to the Living Tribunal: a giant three-faced humanoid cosmic being whose purpose is to keep the multiverse in balance. In the comic books, the Wand of Watoomb is controlled by thought and grants the user near-omnipotent power. The Vaulting Boots of Valtorr is a reference to Valtorr, a mystical entity.

The film depicts the Orb of Agamotto as a large spherical object that allows the sorcerers at Kamar-Taj to observe the protective shield that surrounds the Earth. In the comics, it's a much smaller scrying ball, which Doctor Strange uses to detect the use of magic around the world and observe other dimensions. In the source material, Agamotto is an early practitioner of the mystic arts. He, along with Hoggoth and Oshtur, form the Vishanti, a group that guards the Earth from mystical threats. The symbol adorning the New York Sanctum's oculus is known in the source material as the Seal of the Vishanti, which casts a protective spell over the building.

As Dormammu transports Kaecilius and his Zealots from Earth, he transforms them into Mindless Ones. In the comics, the Mindless Ones are savage creatures that attack other living beings. They possess no will of their own and are often controlled by others.

In the mid-credits scene, we see Doctor Strange wearing orange gloves, a piece of clothing that his comic book counterpart is often seen wearing.

MCU Easter Eggs

Avengers Tower can be spotted in aerial shots of New York. When the Ancient One sends Stephen Strange on a journey through several dimensions, one of the ones he visits is the Quantum Realm. Thor pays Doctor Strange a visit in the mid-credits scene.

Chopped, Changed, and Lengthened

- Derrickson has revealed that a version of the script had a line in which Doctor Strange points out to Dormammu that he's killed Strange over a thousand times during the time loop.
- Drafts of the script had Stephen Strange become the Sorcerer Supreme by the end of the film. The idea was ultimately scrapped as it was felt it was too early for the character to take up the mantle.
- A prologue taking place at CERN ended up not being used. Though what happens in the scene has not been revealed, Kevin Feige has drawn parallels between scientific research done on alternate realities and the lessons the Ancient One teaches Stephen.
- A scene was shot showing the death of Stephen's sister (Lulu Wilson was cast in the role), who drowned at a young age. The sequence didn't work with the rest of the film and so was cut.
- Whilst searching for Kamar-Taj, Stephen walks down a deserted street and comes across an injured dog. He creates a splint for the canine's leg after which it walks away. Stephen is then confronted by several men who intend to rob him.
- Upon arriving at Kamar-Taj, Mordo leads Stephen through the courtyard where we see people training as well as some using electronic devices. The pair then arrive at the Ancient One's sanctuary.
- Entering the New York Sanctum for the first time, Stephen finds Master Drumm who warns him of the impending arrival of Kaecilius and his Zealots. Telling Stephen to stay where he is, Drumm grabs a weapon and walks away.

- Kaecilius enters a chapel. He recites a Bible passage and points out how the afterlife is a contradiction to the priest, before killing him. Kaecilius and his Zealots then complete the second ritual from the Book of Cagliostro.
- Kaecilius and his Zealots enter an abandoned church. A nervous male Zealot questions whether or not Kaecilius has deciphered the Cagliostro ritual correctly, with Kaecilius replying that if he's wrong then Dormammu will simply ignore them. They all begin chanting, after which we find all of them gaining power from the Dark Dimension (with Dormammu's symbol appearing on their forehead) except for the aforementioned nervous Zealot. Noticing this, Kaecilius kills him.
- An alternate ending sees Wong and Stephen in the New York Sanctum. Stephen notes that there has still been no word on Mordo's whereabouts to which Wong replies, "He'll return when he's ready. As the Stones sang, 'Time is on our side'" (referring to the Rolling Stones). Stephen then proceeds to correct him, saying that it was written by Jerry Ragovoy (under the pseudonym Norman Meade) and was first recorded by Kai Winding. Wong then notes that singer Irma Thomas also released a version of it before the Rolling Stones, a fact that Stephen admits he didn't know. Stephen then moves to the oculus window and looks at his broken watch.

Location, Location

Having stolen pages from the Book of Cagliostro, Kaecilius and his zealots are discovered by the Ancient One. They quickly make their escape to London via the **London Sanctum**. The doors they walk out of are those of the National Liberal Club (1 Whitehall Place). Running down **Northumberland Avenue**, they encounter the Ancient One again where the avenue intersects with Great Scotland Yard. After a fight in the Mirror Dimension, Kaecilius flees, with the Ancient One walking back onto Northumberland Avenue and heading in the direction of Trafalgar Square.

For Stephen Strange's **hospital** workplace, the filmmakers used sets built at Longcross Film Studios (Chobham Lane, Chertsey, Surrey) and combined it with Londoneast-uk Business and Technical Park (Yew Tree Avenue, Dagenham) in East London, which stood in for the corridors and operating theatres. The building at 353 West End Avenue, New York City, serves as the exterior to **Stephen Strange's apartment**, with the interior being a constructed set. On his way to the Neurological Society dinner, Stephen drives over the **George**

Washington Bridge. A section of the River Thames doubled for the **Hudson River** where Stephen has a car accident, injuring his hands. The shoreline used can be found in Northfleet, a town in Kent, England. Stephen finds Jonathan Pangborn at a **basketball court**. Although it appears the location could be somewhere in The Bronx, it's actually London's Royal Oak Skatepark, found underneath the A40 Westway.

Stephen then travels to Nepal in a last-ditch effort to find a way to heal himself, with some filming actually conducted on location. We see Stephen visit **Pashupatinath Temple** (Pashupati Nath Road 44621, Kathmandu) before asking around for directions at the Buddhist complex of **Swayambhunath**. Moving south of Kathmandu, an aerial shot of **Patan Durbar Square** in Patan (also known as Lalitpur) is shown before Stephen is robbed in an alley.

Patan Durbar Square

The **chapel** in which Kaecilius and the Zealots perform a ritual from the Book of Cagliostro is the Exeter College Chapel (Turl Street, Oxford, England). When Stephen walks out of the New York Sanctum for the first time and onto **Bleecker Street**, it's actually New York's W 12th Street he's stepping onto (intersecting W Fourth Street) with the Sanctum digitally replacing the wall that's actually there. After a scuffle with Kaecilius, Stephen and Mordo are chased out onto the streets. They stop on **Madison Avenue** in front of the boutique hotel The James New York – NoMad (22 E 29th Street, New York), with Kaecilius and his zealots running towards them down Madison Avenue through the intersection at E 30th Street. Stephen and Mordo try to escape through a portal at the **E 32nd Street and Madison Avenue intersection** but are thwarted when Kaecilius manipulates the landscape. Another fight takes place during which the Ancient One is mortally wounded, and she ends up falling in front of a **glass building**. While it's still meant to be New York, in actual fact this segment was filmed in London, in front of the Costa Coffee that's located in CityPoint (1 Ropemaker Street).

A **Kathmandu street**, **Kamar-Taj**, the **New York Sanctum Sanctorum**, and the 570-foot (174-metre) long **Hong Kong street** were all built as sets at Longcross Film Studios in the UK. Though none of the action was actually filmed in Hong Kong, aerial footage of the city was completed. The design of the **Hong Kong Sanctum** appears to be based on the Lui Seng Chun building located at 119 Lai Chi Kok Road, Mong Kok, Hong Kong.

GUARDIANS OF THE GALAXY VOL. 2

Director: James Gunn
Screenplay: James Gunn

Producer: Kevin Feige
Executive Producers: Nikolas Korda, Stan Lee, Jonathan Schwartz, Victoria Alonso, and Louis D'Esposito
Co-Producers: David J Grant and Lars P Winther
Associate Producer: Simon Hatt

Cinematography: Henry Braham
Production Design: Scott Chambliss
Editing: Fred Raskin and Craig Wood
Music: Tyler Bates
Costume Design: Judianna Makovsky
Visual Effects Supervisor: Christopher Townsend
Casting: Sarah Halley Finn

Production Company: Marvel Studios
Distribution Company: Walt Disney Studios Motion Pictures

US Release Date: 5 May 2017
Running Time: 136 minutes
Budget: $200 million
Box Office: $863,756,051

Based on the Marvel Comics by Dan Abnett and Andy Lanning

Cast: Chris Pratt (*Peter Quill/Star-Lord*), Zoe Saldana (*Gamora*), Dave Bautista (*Drax*), Vin Diesel (*Baby Groot*), Bradley Cooper (*Rocket*), Michael Rooker (*Yondu*), Karen Gillan (*Nebula*), Pom Klementieff (*Mantis*), Sylvester Stallone (*Stakar Ogord*), Kurt Russell (*Ego*), Elizabeth Debicki (*Ayesha*), Chris Sullivan (*Taserface*), Sean Gunn (*Kraglin* and *On-Set Rocket*), Tommy Flanagan (*Tullk*), Laura Haddock (*Meredith Quill*), Ben Browder (*Sovereign Admiral*), Alex Klein (*Zylak*), Evan Jones (*Retch*), Joe Fria (*Oblo*), Terence Rosemore (*Narblik*), Jimmy Urine (*Halfnut*), Stephen Blackehart (*Brahl*), Steve Agee (*Gef*), Blondy Baruti (*Huhtar*), Richard Christy (*"Down There!"*), Rob Zombie (*Unseen Ravager*), Seth Green (*Howard the Duck*), Michael Rosenbaum (*Martinex*), Rhoda Griffis (*Sneeper Madame*), Stan Lee (*Watcher Informant*), David Hasselhoff (*The Form of David Hasselhoff*), Mac Wells (*Officer Fitzgibbon*), James Gunn Sr (*Weird Old Man*), Leota Gunn (*Weird Old Man's Mistress*), Wyatt Oleff (*Young Peter Quill*), Gregg Henry (*Grandpa Quill*), Ving Rhames (*Charlie-27*), Michelle Yeoh (*Aleta Ogord*), Miley Cyrus (*Mainframe*), Jeff Goldblum (*Grandmaster*)

As the Guardians of the Galaxy continue their adventures through space, the team must learn how to work together as a family, while Peter Quill grapples with the appearance of his biological father, the mysterious Ego.

Even before *Guardians of the Galaxy* (2014) hit theatres, director and writer James Gunn knew what he wanted to explore in the sequel. Gunn conceived the story of Peter Quill's father and why Yondu kidnapped Quill as he was writing the first *Guardians* film, concepts that would be a focal point in *Guardians of the Galaxy Vol. 2*.

The core five Guardians would return, although one member wouldn't appear as he did in the first instalment. Originally, Gunn was to have depicted Groot as an adult again, having grown from the sapling state he was left in from the previous film. However, he found this concept repetitive and chose to have the character remain a baby instead. To allow for this, Gunn set the sequel a few months after the events of the first *Guardians of the Galaxy*. The Ravagers, led by Michael Rooker's Yondu Udonta, and Nebula also return, their relationships with Peter Quill and Gamora, respectively, being further explored.

A new Guardians member—Mantis, an insect-like alien with empathic abilities—would be introduced, played by French actress Pom Klementieff. Elizabeth Debicki landed the part of Ayesha, high priestess of the gold-skinned

Sovereign. Casting director Sarah Halley Finn recommended the actress to Gunn, Debicki being only one of two actresses who got to audition—a rarity when many more are usually considered.

Unresolved from the previous film was the identity of Peter Quill's father. Gunn disliked J'son—Quill's father in the comics—due to his royal heritage and, in turn, the comparisons it drew to the *Star Wars* franchise. And so for Quill's dad, the director turned to another character from the source material: Ego. There was one problem: Marvel Studios didn't own the rights to the character. Fortunately, the studio that did—Twentieth Century Fox—were up for a trade. Fox agreed to give Ego to Marvel in exchange for letting them alter the powers of Negasonic Teenage Warhead for the 2016 film *Deadpool* (in the comics she has telepathic and precognitive abilities, on-screen she was given explosive powers). Luckily, the plan worked out given that Gunn did not have a backup character to use in Ego's place. At the suggestion of Chris Pratt, Gunn cast Kurt Russell in the role.

Principal photography began on 17 February 2016 under the working title *Level Up*. Many crew members who worked with Gunn on the first instalment—including cinematographer Ben Davis—were unable to return due to the changed production schedule on *Doctor Strange*. Principal photography concluded on 16 June 2016.

Since dancing Groot at the end of the first *Guardians* film was such a hit with audiences, getting baby Groot right was of utmost importance. While Gunn looked at babies and toddlers as references, he didn't want the young Groot to be too human. A ten-inch (25.4-centimetre) maquette was created and used during filming—both as something for the other actors to work with and a lighting reference for the visual effects team. For the opening title sequence, Gunn's movements were once again used as a reference for Groot as he dances around while the other Guardians of the Galaxy battle an Abilisk.

With this being a sequel, audiences are treated to new worlds as the Guardians visit a range of planets over the course of the film. The design of the gold planet, Sovereign, was based off 1970s Las Vegas as well as the sets from the film *Cleopatra* (1934). While Ayesha's throne room was built as a practical set, a polished gold look was desired and so a digital version was created to replace it. Berhert was built as a 360-degree set with blue screen, and could be lit for both day and night sequences. Real tree trunks were brought in and were digitally extended in post to a height of about forty to fifty feet (twelve to fifteen metres). Mandelbrots and fractals underscored the design of Ego's colourful planet. The design extends to Ego's castle as well, which was designed to evoke Baroque architecture.

Songs played a big part in the first instalment. With Quill having unveiled a second mixtape at the end of that film, songs would also play a pivotal role in *Vol. 2*. Gunn chose tracks that Meredith Quill would have given to her son at a more mature age, adding them into the script as he was writing it. Well-known songs include "Mr Blue Sky" by Electric Light Orchestra, which plays over the opening titles, and Fleetwood Mac's "The Chain," which is used to represent the Guardians and their story. More obscure tracks are also featured, such as "Lake Shore Drive" by Aliotta Haynes Jeremiah. Released in 1971, the song was a hit in the American Midwest—where Gunn grew up—but was otherwise unheard of in other parts of the world. An original track was also created. Written by the Sneepers (the band consisting of Gunn and composer Tyler Bates), the song features David Hasselhoff on vocals, Gunn pitching the idea to the actor after he filmed his part for *Vol. 2*.

On 19 April 2017, *Guardians of the Galaxy Vol. 2* had its world premiere at the Dolby Theatre in Hollywood. Writer and director James Gunn once again dazzled audiences through the combination of a moving story, catchy soundtrack, and spectacular visuals. Earning over $860 million worldwide—more than what the first *Guardians of the Galaxy* film made—Marvel Studios had another hit.

Excelsior!

In his first appearance, a spacesuit-clad Stan Lee recounts the time he was a FedEx deliveryman to some Watchers. Though this was meant to refer to his cameo from *Captain America: Civil War*, that film chronologically takes place after the events of *Guardians of the Galaxy Vol. 2*. Gunn admitted the reference was a mistake on his part. During the shooting of the scene, the director had Lee try out various lines referencing his previous cameos. One had Lee mention his time as a DJ, a nod to his *Deadpool* cameo. Lee appears again in the post-credits scene.

Mid-Credits Scenes

Guardians of the Galaxy Vol. 2 contains several mid-credits scenes. The first technically takes place before the credits (it does appear after the "Guardians of the Galaxy will return" message, however). We see Kraglin wearing Yondu's fin, practising his whistling to control a yaka arrow. He ends up losing control and accidentally impales Drax. The second depicts the Ravagers Stakar Ogord, Aleta Ogord, Martinex, Charlie-27, Mainframe, and Krugarr reuniting in the wake of Yondu's death. In the third, Ayesha reveals a new birthing pod that she's created, claiming that the being inside will be able to destroy the Guardians of the Galaxy. She names him Adam. In the final one, Peter Quill walks into adolescent Groot's room and chastises him for not cleaning his room and constantly playing video games.

Post-Credits Scene

The three Watchers walk away from Stan Lee, who points out that they were meant to take him home and that he still has more stories to tell.

Marvellous Miscellanea

- Gunn wrote a special Groot version of the script, translating every instance of "I am Groot" into English. Gunn and Vin Diesel were the only ones with access to it.
- Edgar Wright contacted Gunn to ensure that his film *Baby Driver* (2017) wouldn't use any of the same songs as *Vol. 2*. Both movies feature songs heavily within the plot, though *Baby Driver* sees the titular character time his movements to the songs he listens to. While neither director revealed exactly what songs they were planning to use, each did reveal the names of the artists in question, from which they discovered there was no overlap.
- The license plate on Ego's 1979 Ford Mustang Cobra—"PZM 569"—is the same one Gunn had on the Buick Electra he drove in high school. Speaking of the Mustang, the car's teal and orange colour scheme echoes that of the *Milano*.
- To aid in the de-ageing of Kurt Russell, Lola Visual Effects used the actor's appearance from the Robert Zemeckis-directed film *Used Cars* (1980) as a reference.
- The device Peter Quill uses to track the Abilisk is a Mattel Electronics Classic Football game.
- A new type of appliance called Pros-Aide was used for Drax's tattoos that greatly aided the makeup process. While it originally took over four hours to get Bautista to look like Drax on the first *Guardians* film, the entire procedure for *Vol. 2* took two-and-a-half hours at first, which was reduced to approximately one-and-a-half hours. To facilitate the

easy removal of the appliances, Bautista had to sit in a portable sauna after filming was complete each day, with the pieces coming off as the actor sweat.
- For this instalment, Vin Diesel recorded Groot's lines in sixteen different languages.
- The large alien words on Peter Quill's shirt translate to "Gears Shift," a brand of candy in the MCU galaxy. The words underneath translate to "A Teneyck Galaxy Invention," a nod to Karen TenEyck, a graphic designer who worked on the film. The small words on the right are "Dust," "Cement," "Stone," and "Ash."
- The scene in which Gamora is attacked by Nebula in an M-ship is a homage to the crop duster scene from *North by Northwest* (1959).
- In every film he's directed, James Gunn has named a character Fitzgibbon after his friend Larry Fitzgibbon: in *Slither* (2006), he's played by Michael Cromien; in *Super* (2010), it's William Katt as Sergeant Fitzgibbon; in *Guardians of the Galaxy*, it's a Dr Fitzgibbon (Robert Firth) in the film's opening; while in *Guardians of the Galaxy Vol. 2*, we have Officer Fitzgibbon played by Mac Wells.
- Many members of Gunn's family make cameo appearances in the film. His parents, James Gunn Sr and Leota Gunn, are taking pictures of the giant blue mass on Earth. Grace, his niece, portrays a pink girl, the first sentient being Ego meets (seen during his telling of his origin). His brother-in-law and his nephew, Griffin, appear as Aakons, running away from Ego's destruction. James Gunn's dog, Wesley Von Spears, appears in the back of a truck at the Dairy Queen parking lot. The dog's owner in the film is played by Gunn's assistant on *Vol. 2*, Jake Martin.
- Other people who make cameos include Jimmy Urine (lead singer of Mindless Self Indulgence), who plays a Ravager named Halfnut; drummer and radio personality Richard Christy who portrays the Ravager that shouts "Down there!" when Yondu kills the crew members that mutinied against him; and Guillermo Rodriguez, Jimmy Kimmel's sidekick on *Jimmy Kimmel Live!* (2003-), who plays a police officer briefly spotted when the giant blue mass expands for the second time on Earth.
- Gunn tries to use the names of actual alien species from the comics in the film where possible. When attempting to get the Sneeper species cleared, Marvel's legal department advised the director that it shouldn't be used, as its pronunciation is similar to *snípur*, the Icelandic word for

clitoris. After all the attention this got on the internet, the legal department conceded it wouldn't be a big issue and allowed its use.
- Microsoft weren't very happy about the Zune's inclusion in the film and how it's initially used as a joke. And yet, knowing that they would inflate in price after the film's release, Gunn bought several of the discontinued media players off eBay and had some signed by himself and the cast. One was auctioned off for charity with the proceeds going to Rainforest Trust.
- There are some words written in the Skrull language in adolescent Groot's room. The one by the door reads "FUCK YOU," while the one on the wall translates to "Maple." The former is unsurprising, with Gunn revealing that baby Groot says the word "fuck" roughly fifty times over the course of the film.
- Like the first *Guardians* film, a message in the credits reads: "No raccoons or tree creatures were harmed during the making of this feature." Another sentence has been added this time around: "The same cannot be said for handlers of said raccoons and tree creatures."

From Panels to the Screen

The Groot of the Marvel Cinematic Universe doesn't appear to grow as fast as his comic book counterpart—he's still a baby after two months, whereas in the comics he can grow from a splinter to his adult form in a relatively short amount of time. Yondu acquires a new, larger fin in the film, reflective of the one the Earth-691 version has in the comics.

Early on, we're introduced to the golden-skinned Ayesha. In the source material, the character has also gone by the names Kismet, Her, and Paragon. She was created by the Enclave as a genetically perfect life form—a status that's bestowed upon the entire Sovereign race in the movie. In one of the mid-credits scenes, Ayesha reveals that she has created something that could defeat the Guardians, dubbing him "Adam." This is a reference to the character Adam Warlock, an artificial creation designed to be the perfect human. He can encase himself in a cocoon, allowing him to heal (hence the gold sarcophagus). Adam was actually created by the Enclave first, with Her/Ayesha coming about after Adam escaped.

In the comics, Ego is known as the Living Planet and, as his name implies, is a planet with sentience. He was created by the Stranger, his consciousness not having developed naturally as previously believed. Unlike the cinematic version, Ego is not a Celestial in the source material, with the biggest deviation being his status as Peter Quill's biological father (in the comics, it's J'son, Emperor of the Spartoi Empire). While Ego cannot take on human form himself, he can create humanoid anti-bodies, communicate using telepathy, and has control over every one of his molecules. In the film, Ego wishes to transform other planets into extensions of himself. A similar event has occurred in the comics: when Tana Nile bonded a part of Ego to another planet in an attempt to terraform it, Ego-Prime was created, a human-shaped entity with its own consciousness. In *Thor* #202 (1972), Ego-Prime reveals his plan to have all of humanity merge with the Earth, converting it into a sentient planet like Ego.

Mantis' background in the film deviates greatly from the comics. In the source material, she's a human of German and Vietnamese descent, the daughter of Gustav Brandt and Lau Nguyen Brandt. She grew up under the care of the Priests of Pama (exiled pacifist members of the Kree race) who believed she would grow up to be the Celestial Madonna and give birth to the Celestial Messiah. A skilled martial artist, Mantis also possesses empathic abilities, telepathy, limited precognition, and astral projection. She first joined the Avengers before becoming a member of the Guardians of the Galaxy in *Guardians of the Galaxy* #1 (2008). The cinematic incarnation of the character has light-coloured skin in keeping with the comic book version's early appearances. Though she appears green nowadays in the source material, she can change her skin colour as she pleases.

The Guardians properly meet Ego on a planet called Berhert, which is home to the Sagittarians in the comics. The planet the Ravagers relax on is Contraxia, a planet in the Elidra star system in the source material, where it constantly snows and is home to the Contraxians. A painting of Wal Rus can be seen in the room Yondu occupies at the Iron Lotus. In the comics, Wal Rus is a walrus that hails from Halfworld, the same place Rocket Raccoon is from. The alien in charge of the Iron Lotus is identified in the credits as a Sneeper. In the comics, Sneepers are a green skinned, semi-humanoid alien race from the planet Sneep.

Believe it or not, Taserface is an actual character from the comics, although the cinematic incarnation bears no resemblance to his comic book counterpart who is a cyborg and scout for the Stark. Both versions, however, do come to blows with the Guardians of the Galaxy. Other Ravagers with names taken from the comics include Brahl (a member of the Minions of Menace in the source material) and Tullk (a green-skinned galactic bounty hunter in the source material).

Several planets seen on Rocket's screen as the Quadrant detaches from the *Eclector* come from the comics. Drez-Lar and Terma are planets part of the Kree Empire, while Hala is home to the Kree. While unidentified on-screen, when Ego's seeds sprout and expand, we see some Aakons running on what is presumably their home planet, which in the comics is known as Oorga.

Stan Lee appears in the film talking to some bald figures with large heads. The characters are known as Watchers, with their species observing and recording the events of the universe, vowing to never interfere. The most well-known Watcher in the comics is Uatu, who keeps an eye on Earth and its solar system.

Though we see the individual characters throughout the film, in a mid-credits scene we witness Stakar Ogord assembling other Ravager leaders together. This is a reference to the original Guardians team of the comics. The characters present are Stakar (also known as Starhawk, who generates light energy and possesses a vast intellect), Krugarr (Doctor Strange's successor in Earth-691), Charlie-27 (possesses enhanced strength and durability; he is Caucasian in the comics), Aleta Ogord (Stakar's adoptive sister, who merged with him to become Starhawk), Martinex (who has a body made of silicon crystal and can emit blasts of heat and cold from his hands), and Mainframe (an alternate version of the Vision hailing from Earth-691). The original Guardians lineup in the comics was composed of Charlie-27, Martinex, Vance Astro, and Yondu.

MCU Easter Eggs

Howard the Duck once again makes an appearance (he can be seen on the ice planet Contraxia). During the credits, an image of Cosmo can be spotted, as well as a dancing Grandmaster (a character from the then-unreleased *Thor: Ragnarok*).

Chopped, Changed, and Lengthened

- Gunn had included Adam Warlock in the treatment for the film but found that there were too many characters and he couldn't service them all properly. He decided to use Adam in the next instalment.
- A scene set on Earth was filmed which would have contained Nathan Fillion's cameo. Gunn had Fillion portray Simon Williams, with the character adorning several posters that were displayed outside a theatre in the film as part of a Simon Williams Film Festival. (In the comics, Simon Williams is an actor and a superhero going by the name Wonder

Man.) Each movie poster itself was an Easter egg. The one for *Tony Stark* parodies the *Steve Jobs* (2015) poster, *Dead Before Arrival* is a nod to *Inception* (2010), *Haxan 2* mirrors *Horns* (2013), *Oh, Rebecca!* resembles the poster for *Definitely, Maybe* (2008), *Arkon*—a Marvel Comics character—is a reference to *Conan the Barbarian* (1982), and *Toxic Janitor 2* is a ringer for *The Toxic Avenger* (1984) poster. The scene also featured storefronts that referenced several comic book artists and writers, such as Starlin Furniture in homage to Jim Starlin. Unfortunately, it was cut as it slowed the film's pace.

- After Drax tells Quill, "You just need to find a woman who is pathetic. Like you," Drax hugs him, despite Quill saying he didn't want one.
- Captured and held on board the *Milano*, Nebula calls Gamora a "Garden of the Galaxy," which Gamora corrects.
- Gathered around the campfire on Berhert, the Guardians are visibly annoyed and disgusted over Drax's loud eating.
- After Gef asks Taserface if he can smash baby Groot with a rock and is denied, he says, "Well can I at least poke its eyes out?"
- Showing Quill, Gamora, and Drax around his planet, Ego reveals a memorial he's created to commemorate the war on Xandar. Playing to Quill's ego, the sculpture depicts a muscular Quill holding a sword and standing on top of a defeated Ronan. Gamora is holding on to Quill's leg, Groot is depicted as if he were an actual tree with arms, and Drax is rendered as a small, monkey-like being on Quill's shoulder.
- Drax's conversation with Mantis on Ego's planet was originally longer. When Mantis touches Drax and experiences his emotions, she tells him that she's never felt love like the kind the Guardians have for each other before and notes that "It both hurts and soothes the heart." Gunn found that by cutting this segment the scene was more impactful, with audiences paying attention to the expressions on the characters' faces.
- During the expansion of Ego's giant blue mass on Earth, Peter Quill's grandfather rescues a woman and escapes with her in a car. The scene was cut as Gunn felt audiences preferred seeing the Guardians go up against Ego.
- A version in which Yondu says, "I'm Mary Poppins, motherfuckers!" was filmed.
- Alternate lines Drax says after Mantis is knocked out by a piece of debris include "I know; that almost hit me," and "Look out!" immediately fol-

lowed by turning to the others and saying, "I tried guys."
- Gunn has revealed that Glenn Close filmed a cameo reprising her role as Nova Prime that was cut.
- Gunn revealed on Twitter that after Rocket says to Groot, "We're gonna need to have a real discussion about your language," Rocket would have continued with, "'Fuck this, fuck that,' everything's 'fuck fuck fuck' all the time!" The sequence was animated in post-visualization and was never intended to be used in the film.
- Quill's speech at Yondu's funeral was shot twice. Thinking about the scene the night after shooting, Gunn felt that Quill wasn't distraught enough, since Yondu's death took place not too long before his cremation. For the reshoot, Pratt was filmed against blue screen and inserted into what was already shot.
- Kraglin shows Quill how to use the Zune, noting its primitive design and pointing out some of his favourite artists such as the "lady on there named Alice Cooper."
- A longer mid-credits scene with Peter Quill and adolescent Groot was filmed. After being told he's boring, in an effort to prove otherwise, Quill recounts the time he was on a planet where the inhabitants were lines and dots, how he and Drax switched pants at a party, that he's killed thousands of aliens, the time he saved the galaxy with a dance-off, and how he once contracted a venereal disease that caused him to float for several days.
- An additional tag scene was filmed. Gamora and Mantis are talking on the Quadrant when they hear a scream. The scene would have then cut to Gef, revealing that he's injured but still alive. The sequence was removed, as there wasn't a good reason or need to refer back to the character.

Location, Location

This time around, the production was based at Pinewood Atlanta Studios (461 Sandy Creek Road, Fayetteville, Georgia), now known as Trilith Studios. Opening with a flashback to 1980, we see Ego and Meredith Quill driving down what is meant to be a **road in Missouri**. In actuality, it's a section of Brandon Farm Road SW, Georgia. The **Dairy Queen** they drive to can be found at 5039 Memorial Drive, Stone Mountain, Georgia. The premises no longer host a DQ restaurant.

Sets for the interiors of Yondu's ship, the *Eclector*, were constructed and shot at the Georgia International Convention Center (2000 Convention Center Concourse, College Park, Georgia). Later on, we see **people in the Missouri town running from Ego's growing spore**. This was filmed on E Main Street (between S Railroad Street and S Gilmer Street) in Cartersville, Georgia. With the blue mass having momentarily stopped growing, **people have gathered near it to take photos**. This was shot nearby on S Public Square. We then see **the mass slowly push a car forward before stopping**. This was shot on N Wall Street in front of Ross' Diner (17 N Wall Street, Cartersville).

SPIDER-MAN: HOMECOMING

Director: Jon Watts
Screenplay: Jonathan Goldstein & John Francis Daley and
Jon Watts & Christopher Ford and Chris McKenna & Erik Sommers
Story: Jonathan Goldstein & John Francis Daley

Producers: Kevin Feige and Amy Pascal
Executive Producers: Louis D'Esposito, Victoria Alonso, Patricia Whitcher,
Jeremy Latcham, Stan Lee, Avi Arad, and Matt Tolmach
Co-Producers: Mitch Bell, Eric Hauserman Carroll, and Rachel O'Connor

Cinematography: Salvatore Totino
Production Design: Oliver Scholl
Editing: Dan Lebental and Debbie Berman
Music: Michael Giacchino
Costume Design: Louise Frogley
Visual Effects Supervisor: Janek Sirrs
Casting: Sarah Halley Finn

Production Companies: Pascal Pictures, Marvel Studios, and Columbia Pictures
Distribution Company: Sony Pictures Releasing

US Release Date: 7 July 2017
Running Time: 133 minutes
Budget: $175 million
Box Office: $880,166,924

Based on the Marvel Comics by Stan Lee and Steve Ditko

Cast: Tom Holland (*Peter Parker/Spider-Man*), Michael Keaton (*Adrian Toomes/Vulture*), Robert Downey Jr (*Tony Stark/Iron Man*), Marisa Tomei (*May Parker*), Jon Favreau (*Happy Hogan*), Gwyneth Paltrow (*Pepper Potts*), Zendaya (*Michelle*), Donald Glover (*Aaron Davis*), Jacob Batalon (*Ned*), Laura Harrier (*Liz*), Tony Revolori (*Flash*), Bokeem Woodbine (*Herman Schultz/Shocker #2*), Tyne Daly (*Anne Marie Hoag*), Abraham Attah (*Abe*), Hannibal Buress (*Coach Wilson*), Kenneth Choi (*Principal Morita*), Selenis Leyva (*Ms Warren*), Angourie Rice (*Betty*), Martin Starr (*Mr Harrington*), Garcelle Beauvais (*Doris Toomes*), Michael Chernus (*Phineas Mason/Tinkerer*), Michael Mando (*Mac Gargan*), Logan Marshall-Green (*Jackson Brice/Shocker #1*), Jennifer Connelly (*Karen*), Jorge Lendeborg Jr (*Jason Ionello*), Tiffany Espensen (*Cindy*), Isabella Amara (*Sally*), Michael Barbieri (*Charles*), JJ Totah (*Seymour*), Hemky Madera (*Mr Delmar*), Zach Cherry (*Street Vendor*), Stan Lee (*Gary*), Chris Evans (*Steve Rogers/Captain America*), Kerry Condon (*FRIDAY*), Ethan Dizon (*Tiny*)

Teenager Peter Parker learns to juggle being a student and his responsibilities as Spider-Man under the mentorship of Tony Stark. His life soon becomes complicated as he tries to stop the sale of illegal weapons and the emergence of the Vulture.

The Amazing Spider-Man 2 was released on 2 May 2014. The film—a sequel in the newly rebooted Spider-Man film franchise—was, by the end of its run, the lowest grossing Spider-Man instalment. The two Spider-Man movies directed by Marc Webb were to start an interconnected franchise featuring the Marvel characters whose cinematic rights belonged to Sony Pictures Entertainment: a third and fourth Spidey movie was planned for release in 2016 and 2018; *Sinister Six* was developed with Drew Goddard; Venom would have gotten his own film (the 2018 *Venom* film is not connected to Webb's two Spider-Man entries); and a yet-to-be-revealed female character would have gotten a film as well. All were suddenly derailed. While the studio had access to the Spider-Man family of characters—of which there are over 900—in perpetuity under the deal it signed in 1999, it was under the condition that they release a new entry every five years and nine months. It seems the studio hadn't learnt from the problems of *Spider-Man 3* (2007), which suffered from too many villains and storylines.

What initially appeared to be a bump in the road would eventually lead to the Spider-Man series being rebooted again, although this time it would be a part of the Marvel Cinematic Universe. Leaked emails from the Sony Pictures Entertainment hack in late 2014 revealed discussions were had between heads at Sony and Disney about the possibility of having Spider-Man appear in *Captain America: Civil War* along with the production of a new trilogy. Sony would retain creative control and the rights to the character, while Marvel Studios would use Spidey in their shared universe. Negotiations allegedly broke down, but in February 2015 it was announced that the two studios had come to an agreement. Marvel would be allowed to use Spider-Man in their crossover films, although Sony wouldn't see a percentage of any profits made. Conversely, Disney would not receive more than five percent of the first-dollar gross from each instalment in Sony's new trilogy (it was initially reported that Disney would not receive any of the revenue from the new trilogy), which would be produced by Kevin Feige and former Sony Pictures co-chairperson Amy Pascal. Marvel had creative freedom to take Spider-Man in a direction they saw fit, but Sony had the final say.

Though seemingly simple enough, the arrangement was actually more complex. In a 2011 deal, Sony gave up its share of Spider-Man merchandising rights to Disney, while Disney relinquished their five percent take of the revenue from each Spider-Man film (a clause that was in place when Marvel licenced the cinematic rights of Spider-Man to Sony). The same agreement also saw Disney hand Sony a one-off payment of $175 million and up to $35 million for every future Spidey instalment. With their unprecedented partnership, however, this arrangement was modified, allowing Marvel to reduce its $35 million payment should *Spider-Man: Homecoming* gross over $750 million. Marvel would also be paid a producer's fee (the exact figure hasn't been disclosed).

Over 1,500 actors were looked at for the coveted role of Peter Parker/Spider-Man, but in the end, Tom Holland won the part. He debuted in *Captain America: Civil War* before starring in Spider-Man's solo film. Around the same time as the search for a new Spider-Man actor was underway, a director for the franchise was also sought. Jon Watts was hired to helm the Spider-Man reboot, with his critically acclaimed 2015 film *Cop Car* putting him on Marvel Studios' radar. Watts wanted to create a coming-of-age film, which dovetailed nicely with Marvel's desire to firmly place Peter Parker in high school. The film's tone (several John Hughes movies served as inspiration) and the lack of an origin story would help differentiate the movie from past Spider-Man entries. Other directors who were considered included Jared Hess, Jonathan Levine, Theodore Melfi, and directing duo John Francis Daley and Jonathan M Goldstein.

With the film's high school setting, Watts was determined to populate it with a diverse cast, reflecting the varied ethnicities of students attending New York schools. To that end, Jacob Batalon, who has a Filipino background, was cast as Peter's best friend, Ned; Laura Harrier (whose father is African American and mother English and Polish) was cast as Peter's love interest, Liz; while Guatemalan American Tony Revolori won the role of Flash Thompson, a rival and bully of Peter's. Actress and singer Zendaya was cast as Michelle. To prepare them, Watts had the young actors watch coming-of-age movies, such as *The Breakfast Club* (1985), *Ferris Bueller's Day Off* (1986), *Say Anything…* (1989), as well as the television show *Freaks and Geeks* (1999-2000).

To help cement the film as a part of the MCU—and act as a commercial boon for the film—Robert Downey Jr as Tony Stark and Jon Favreau's Happy Hogan were added to the main cast, allowing the filmmakers to continue the relationship between Tony and Peter established in *Civil War*.

For the role of Adrian Toomes/Vulture, Feige and Pascal turned to a veteran of the comic book movie genre: Michael Keaton. Keaton previously played Batman in *Batman* (1989) and *Batman Returns* (1992). Initially, scheduling conflicts with *The Founder* (2016) prevented the actor from accepting the role, but a subsequent change in that film's schedule meant he could take part. The Vulture wouldn't be the only villain from the comics to appear in the film, with Michael Chernus cast as Phineas Mason/Tinkerer and Logan Marshall-Green and Bokeem Woodbine both portraying incarnations of the Shocker.

Principal photography on *Homecoming* began on 20 June 2016 and wrapped over three months later, on 2 October. The film had its world premiere at Grauman's Chinese Theatre in Hollywood on 28 June 2017.

Financially, *Spider-Man: Homecoming* made over $330 million domestically and over $880 million worldwide. Critically, the film was well-received, with praise for Holland's youthful take on the web-slinger and Keaton's multifaceted antagonist. With its light tone and youthful energy, the film aptly shows how a beloved character can be, once again, reinterpreted and presented in a fresh way. For Sony, teaming up with Marvel Studios and rebooting the Spider-Man franchise so soon after the *The Amazing Spider-Man 2* proved to be the right thing to do.

Excelsior!

Stan Lee plays Gary, one of the apartment tenants who appears during Spider-Man's attempt to thwart a carjacking.

Mid-Credits Scene
In prison, Mac Gargan approaches Adrian Toomes and asks him if he knows Spider-Man's real identity. Adrian replies that if he did, Spider-Man would already be dead.

Post-Credits Scene
Captain America appears on-screen to espouse the virtues of patience. He notes that sometimes it can lead to victory, while at other times it can leave one feeling disappointed for having waited so long for very little.

Marvellous Miscellanea
- As Holland went to an all-boys school in London, he covertly attended The Bronx High School of Science for a couple of days to get an idea of what it was like being a high school student in New York. He went by the name Ben Perkins, a nod to his acting coach from *The Impossible* (2012).
- In recognition of playing Spider-Man, Holland got a spider symbol tattoo at the bottom of his right foot.
- The working title used during production was *Summer of George*, a reference to the *Seinfeld* (1989-98) episode of the same name.
- An orchestral version of the 1967-70 *Spider-Man* animated series theme song is played over the Marvel Studios logo instead of the usual fanfare.
- When Peter is viewing the "Amazing Man-Spider saves bus full of kids!" video on YouTube, some of the recommended videos are for a channel called "waverlyflams." It's a real channel and belongs to Waverly Films, a group of filmmakers that includes Jon Watts.
- Kirk Thatcher appears as the punk in the film who carries a boom box and stands next to the hotdog vendor. This is a nod to his role in *Star Trek IV: The Voyage Home* (1986) in which Thatcher plays a punk who plays loud music on the bus. The idea came about when Kevin Feige discovered he and Thatcher were going to be in New York during the last days of shooting *Homecoming*. Feige—who's a huge *Star Trek* fan—subsequently offered the actor a cameo role.
- The piece of graffiti that says "Bagley" (seen on a building when Happy tells Spider-Man that Tony sold Avengers tower) is a reference to artist Mark Bagley, known for his work on the *Ultimate Spider-Man* series. Additionally, before Spider-Man crashes Flash's car, the name "McFarlane" can be seen graffitied on a wall. This is a nod to writer and artist

Todd McFarlane who has worked on various Spider-Man titles.
- The crew had seven pre-made Lego Death Stars for filming. This was fortunate, as according to Holland, Batalon kept mistiming the drop and breaking the prop. For those wanting to track down a set, the 3,803-piece model Ned says he has is from 2008 and has the item number 10188.
- During gym class, Michelle can be seen reading *Of Human Bondage* by W Somerset Maugham. In the novel, the protagonist, Philip Carey, is orphaned and sent to live with his aunt and uncle, which is what happens with Peter Parker.
- Before Andrew Garfield was cast as Peter Parker in *The Amazing Spider-Man* (2012), Donald Glover actively campaigned for the role. Though he didn't get the part, his campaign was referenced in the first episode of the second season of *Community* (2009-15), "Anthropology 101." In it, Glover's character, Troy Barnes, can be seen wearing Spider-Man pyjamas. It was this moment that convinced comic book writer Brian Michael Bendis that an African-American Spider-Man would work, with Miles Morales making his debut in *Ultimate Fallout* #4 (2011). Glover would subsequently voice the character in episodes of *Ultimate Spider-Man* (2012-17). His connection to Spider-Man doesn't end there though. In *The Amazing Spider-Man*, a picture of Troy Barnes can be seen in Peter's bedroom, while the clip of Troy in his Spidey PJs can be spotted in *Spider-Man: Into the Spider-Verse* (2018).
- After the Vulture drops Spider-Man into water, he appears silhouetted in front of the moon. This is a reference to the 1989 film *Batman*, in which a similar moment is achieved when Batman flies up into the sky in the Batwing.
- Following Spider-Man's initial confrontation with the Vulture, Tony says to Peter, "Steady, Crockett." This is a reference to the *Miami Vice* (1984-90) character Detective James "Sonny" Crockett who would often defy orders from his superiors.
- The A113 Easter egg can be seen as part of the spider-drone's HUD.
- Though it isn't a part of the MCU, the famous upside-down kiss from *Spider-Man* (2002) is referenced when Karen urges Peter to kiss Liz after he rescues her. And whether intentional or not, when Spider-Man holds the two halves of the Staten Island Ferry together, his pose bears a similarity to the one Tobey Maguire's Spider-Man uses to stop a speeding train in *Spider-Man 2* (2004).

From Panels to the Screen

Adrian Toomes' company is called Bestman Salvage. This is a reference to Adrian's former business partner in the comics, Gregory Bestman, who co-founded Bestman and Toomes Electronics. As per the source material, Damage Control is a company that repairs and cleans up areas in the wake of a fight between superheroes and villains. In both media, Tony Stark is part owner of the company, with Anne Marie Hoag being the director. Tony mentoring a teenage Peter Parker in the film is something that also happened in the comic books, occurring in the Ultimate Universe.

Peter Parker tells Ned that he got his powers from a spider bite, which is exactly how it happened in the comics, as depicted in *Amazing Fantasy* #15 (1962). Other aspects from the character's origin story from this issue aren't touched on, however. For example, with his newfound powers, Peter became a wrestler and later made appearances on television, taking on the name Spider-Man. Returning home one afternoon, Peter finds that an intruder had murdered his Uncle Ben. He locates the killer at a warehouse, discovering that the man was a fleeing burglar he could have stopped at the television studio days earlier. It is in that moment that Peter learned of the responsibility that comes with his powers. The issue is referenced with Aunt May's number plate, which reads "AMF-1562." The film has Peter attend Midtown School of Science & Technology whereas in the comics it's Midtown High School. The school was established in 1962, a nod to the year in which Spidey made his debut. A Piazza New York Mets flag can be seen in Peter's room, indicating that he's a fan, something he has in common with his comic book counterpart. This is revealed in *Peter Parker: Spider-Man* #33 (2001) in which we find out that Uncle Ben often took a young Peter to see the baseball team play.

According to director Jon Watts, the Iron Spider-Man suit from the source material was an indirect inspiration for the Spidey suit in the film. The red and gold costume designed by Tony Stark had audio and visual amplifiers, allowed Peter to glide, and also contained three mechanical arms with cameras on the end. Peter has Ned override the Spider-Man suit's systems, something we find out Peter has done to the Iron Spidey costume in *The Amazing Spider-Man* #536 (2006). The ability for Peter to deploy a drone from his suit may have been inspired by the Spider Armor Mk IV, which has similar capabilities. The web wings are first seen on Steve Ditko's original design of the suit and can be spotted on the cover of *Amazing Fantasy* #15 (1962). We also see Peter use spider-tracers in the film. In the comics, they're devices

Peter created to allow him to track foes as well as allies should they need his help. And while the MCU incarnation of Peter tells Ned he can't summon an army of spiders, Peter (with Otto Octavius in control of his body) has used a bunch of spider-bots to keep an eye on New York City in the source material. In *Spider-Man: Homecoming*, Tony asks Peter to just be a "friendly neighborhood Spider-Man," which is a self-referential phrase Spidey uses in the comics. Peter's homemade suit in the film is based off Ben Reilly's classic Scarlet Spider costume, albeit with the colours reversed (Peter wears a blue sweatshirt and sweatpants with a red hooded vest, while Ben wears a blue hooded vest over red tights).

Peter's friend Ned is named after Ned Leeds. In the comics, Ned didn't go to the same school as Peter, but did work as a reporter at the *Daily Bugle*. He would eventually take on the mantle of the Hobgoblin after being brainwashed by Roderick Kingsley, the original Hobgoblin. His appearance and personality though seem to have been modelled after Ganke—they even included the character's love of Lego!

The character of Liz in the film brings to mind Liz Allan, who's a classmate Peter's from the comics. Though both versions have a mother named Doris and serve as a romantic interest for Peter, in the source material the character is Caucasian with blonde hair and isn't related to Adrian Toomes. The MCU's Flash Thompson bullies Peter just like his comic book counterpart, though he's not a jock and is academically gifted. Instead of teasing Peter with "Puny Parker" (as he does in the comics), he uses "Penis Parker" instead! We see Betty Brandt co-host the school's news program with Jason Ionello. In the comics, Betty worked with Peter at the *Daily Bugle* and was in fact his first girlfriend, while Jason is a fellow student at Midtown High School. Michelle revealing that friends call her "MJ" is an interesting nod to Mary Jane Watson, Peter's most well-known love interest. The connection appears to be in name only, with the comic book incarnation of the character having red hair and an outgoing personality. A student dressed up as Midtown's mascot (a tiger, as it is in the Ultimate Universe), runs past the window before the MJ reveal, bringing to mind what Mary Jane tells Peter when they first meet in *The Amazing Spider-Man* #42 (1966): "Face it, Tiger…you just hit the jackpot!" Charles, Sally, Seymour, and Tiny are possibly named after Charles "Charlie" Murphy, Sally Avril, Seymour O'Reilly, and Brian "Tiny" McKeever, respectively, all of whom attended Midtown High with Peter in the comics. There's also an Asian girl named Cindy, a possible reference to Cindy Moon who in the comic books was bitten by the same spider that gave Peter his powers. Possessing similar abilities to Spider-Man, Cindy goes by the code name "Silk."

Additionally, many of the staff members in the film have counterparts stemming from the comics. Mr Harrington could be a reference to Roger Harrington, principal of Midtown High and the one who hires Peter as a science teacher. Mr Cobbwell may be referring to Professor Cobbwell, an electronics expert whom Peter assisted. Coach Wilson could be a nod to the character of Whiz Wilson, a gym coach at Centerville Junior High School. Shop class teacher Mr Hapgood may have been based off Barry Hapgood, a former classmate of Peter's who, despite his misbehaviour in shop class, became an electronics engineer.

Spider-Man thwarting robbers wearing superhero masks comes from *Ultimate Spider-Man* #42 (2003), though in the issue we see the criminals sport a Captain America, Iron Man, and a Batman mask. Across the road from Delmar's Deli-Grocery is a shop called Kravinoff Exotic. This is a reference to the Spidey villain Sergei Kravinoff, better known as Kraven the Hunter.

Another moment taken from the comics is when Spidey finds that he can't swing around suburban New York due to the lack of tall buildings, occurring in *The Amazing Spider-Man* #267 (1985). The issue is referenced again with the licence plate "ASM-267" which can be seen on the car Spidey jumps over when taking a shortcut through some backyards.

In the comics, Adrian Toomes is an electronics engineer who developed an electromagnetic flying harness. Becoming a thief, he called himself the Vulture. The ruffles on Adrian's jacket in the film is a nod to the Vulture's green comic book costume, which has a feathered collar. Though he's usually depicted as having an exposed head in the suit, the Vulture has on occasion worn a helmet, like the one accompanying his red and black Sinister Twelve outfit. Like the film, the comic book incarnation did indeed have a daughter, though she's named Valeria.

The Phineas Mason/Tinkerer of the Marvel Cinematic Universe is much younger than his comic book counterpart. Both are inventors who create and supply weapons to criminals. A car on the Staten Island Ferry bears the number plate "SM2-0563," referring to *The Amazing Spider-Man* #2 (cover dated May 1963), which features the Vulture's and Tinkerer's first appearance.

We see two incarnations of the Shocker in the film: Jackson Brice and Herman Schultz. The comic book incarnation of Jackson never took on the identity of the Shocker (the character did, though, in the animated television series *The Spectacular Spider-Man*, 2008-09), but was a part of the Enforcers, going by the name Montana and using a lariat as his signature weapon. Herman Schultz was a safecracker who developed two gauntlets that could produce force blasts. Both characters in the film wear an outfit with yellow arms, a signature colour from the Shocker's comic book costume. The licence plate of the van from the weapons sale scene reads "MAR-4667." This is a nod to the Shocker's first appearance in *The Amazing Spider-Man* #46, which has a cover date of March 1967.

The MacDonald "Mac" Gargan of the comics is a private investigator and the first to take on the Scorpion identity, having gained superhuman strength and a full-body suit with a mechanical tail (in the film, the character has a scorpion tattoo on his neck). In the mid-credits scene, Mac tells Adrian Toomes that he knows people outside of prison who would love to meet Spider-Man, a possible reference to the Sinister Six. In the source material, they're a supervillain team composed of Spidey's enemies. The number plate of the white van on the Staten Island Ferry is "SM-1920." This is a dual reference to *The Amazing Spider-Man* #19 (1964) and *The Amazing Spider-Man* #20 (1965), the former being Mac Gargan's first appearance and the latter marking his first appearance as the Scorpion. The car next to it bears the number plate "HTD-003." This is a reference to *Howard the Duck* #3 (2015), an issue that features Aunt May. Additionally, the comic had a variant cover that depicts Howard riding the Staten Island Ferry.

In the comics, Aaron Davis is a master thief from the Ultimate Universe who goes by the name Prowler (which you can see in the film as an alias of his when Karen runs facial recognition, along with the name Brian Pinchelli, referring to writer Brian Michael Bendis and artist Sara Pichelli). During his "interrogation," Aaron tells Spider-Man that he has a nephew. In the source material, Aaron's nephew is Miles Morales—who takes on the mantle of Spider-Man after the death of Peter Parker. Additionally, if you look closely, you can see that Aaron's number plate reads "UCS-M01," referring to *Ultimate Comics Spider-Man* #1 (2011), Aaron Davis' debut issue.

The colour scheme of the Iron Man armour from the Ultimate Universe (a red and gold-coloured suit with silver-coloured lower torso and upper legs) inspired the look of Iron Man's Mark 47 armour in the film. Among other items being moved to the New Avengers facility is Thor's magic belt, Megingjord. In the comics, this item increases Thor's strength when worn.

Spider-Man being trapped under a pile of rubble is a moment taken from

The Amazing Spider-Man #33 (1966). When Peter looks at his reflection in a puddle, we see the iconic split image of Peter and Spidey, something artists would draw whenever Peter's spider-sense was activated. Both the film and comic incarnations of Spider-Man have saved the Vulture when his wing suit malfunctioned. In the source material, this occurs in *The Spectacular Spider-Man* #188 (1992). Additionally, Spidey leaves him all webbed up along with a note, as his comic book counterpart is known to do.

The films ends with Aunt May finding out that Peter is Spider-Man. This is another moment taken from the comics, occurring at the end of *The Amazing Spider-Man* #35 (2001) when May walks in on an injured and sleeping Peter with a tattered Spidey suit next to him.

MCU Easter Eggs

Damage Control takes over the clean-up in the wake of the Battle of New York. The film recounts the airport battle from *Captain America: Civil War* told from Peter Parker's perspective. Captain America appears in several public service announcements shown at the school (with his status as a war criminal being mentioned), and students are taught about the Sokovia Accords. Bank robbers can be seen wearing Iron Man, Captain America, Thor, and Hulk masks. Howard Stark and Abraham Erskine can be seen on a mural at Midtown School of Science & Technology, while a photograph of Bruce Banner can be seen in Peter's classroom. The Tinkerer says that the Shocker's gauntlet came from a clean-up in Lagos, implying that it's a modified version of one of the gauntlets Crossbones used (the other was destroyed when he exploded, remember?). There's a Korean Church of Asgard next to the Thai restaurant May and Peter visit, indicating that some people are worshipping Norse gods in the MCU. Jackson Brice tells Aaron Davis that he's got a weapon crafted from a Sub-Ultron arm, black hole grenades (used by the Dark Elves), and Chitauri railguns for sale.

During the trip to Washington DC, the bus passes a sign informing drivers to use an alternate route due to the Triskelion clean-up. One answer to the decathlon team's practice questions, given by Peter, is "strontium, barium, vibranium." Looking through Vulture's bag, Spidey pulls out a circular metal object (a part of the vibranium detonator Ultron used to lift a chunk of Sokovia into the air), an Ultron head, and a Chitauri energy core. Principal Morita (played by Kenneth Choi) is the grandson of Jim Morita (also played by Kenneth Choi), who was a member of the Howling Commandos; his photograph is on display in the principal's office. Tony sells off Avengers Tower (the robotic Dum-E can be seen helping pack items) and relocates to the New Avengers facility. The Vision is mentioned (along with his habit of phasing through walls), Pepper Potts makes an appearance, and Happy mentions that he's been carrying around Tony's engagement ring since 2008, referring to the year *Iron Man* came out and the debut of the MCU.

Chopped, Changed, and Lengthened

- Marisa Tomei has revealed that a version of the film's script had Aunt May helping a distressed little girl as some sort of incident was occurring in the neighbourhood during an early part of the film.
- The *A film by Peter Parker* segment was originally longer. Peter has a few more interactions with Happy on the private plane, and we see more shots of Peter exploring his Berlin hotel room (he even reveals he brought his homework as he doesn't know how long he'll be away). After returning to the hotel from the airport fight, Peter sneaks out of his room at night wearing his new Spider-Man suit and explores the city before eventually finding a party. The next morning at breakfast, an unamused Happy confronts Peter about his late-night adventure, showing him the current day's newspaper with the headline "Sticky Boy Saves Chancellor."
- Whilst sitting at a table inside the cafeteria, Peter breaks the news to the decathlon team that he won't be going to Washington DC with them. They try to convince him to go, with Liz citing his strength in physics, but Peter isn't convinced and leaves the table. Liz follows him to convince him to attend one last time, but Peter is adamant that he won't.
- After thwarting the ATM robbery, Spidey returns to the alley where he left his bag and clothes only to find them missing. He webs away and stops near the area where he tried to stop a "carjacking." It turns out that the owner is still webbed to his car, with several neighbours keeping him company, with one noting the webbing takes six to seven hours to dissolve. Spider-Man then continues on his way home.
- Peter is on the bus to the decathlon, talking on the phone to Happy, telling him about his trip to Washington DC. The bus then passes several trucks carting items away from the Triskelion clean-up before passing the damaged Triskelion itself.
- Adrian Toomes is in his workshop. His phone rings and he answers it. He speaks to his daughter, telling her how he can fix the broken water

heater and that he'll be home soon. Hanging up, he then pulls down a shelf in frustration.
- We're at the parking lot where Spidey webbed Aaron Davis to his car. Aaron takes his keys out of his pocket but drops them. He tries to retrieve them but can't reach. A woman passes by but refuses to help him. We then cut to Aaron with his keys, trying to use them as a saw to cut the webbing off. Unsuccessful, he calls his nephew, Miles, telling him that he won't make it.
- Peter and Ned walk down the street, close to where the ATM robbery occurred. Peter reassures Ned that he's good to go up against the Vulture again and that he's been practicing with the suit. Ned offers to be Peter's "guy in the chair," but Peter says he needs to do this by himself. They do their unique handshake before heading their separate ways.
- A segment titled *Mr Harrington: Lessons in Love* sees Mr Harrington speak to several people about his ex-wife, Tabitha. He reveals to the bus driver (on the trip to Washington DC) and gym teacher (at the homecoming dance) that Tabitha is a poet and is writing a book, and that he tried therapy but the therapist kept taking Tabitha's side. He even mentions to the Washington Monument tour guide that therapy is a waste of money.
- Inside the now empty Avengers Tower, Happy calls his mother, telling her how Tony entrusted him with the move. Looking out the window, he sees the plane crash near Coney Island. He hangs up on his mum and urgently calls Tony.
- We have a *Midtown News* segment, covering events after the homecoming dance, which includes the following: a message from Principal Morita telling students to remove selfies of a webbed Herman Schultz from their social media accounts; news that the school is installing hand dryers in the bathrooms; Mr Harrington, Michelle, and Ned being asked if they know who Spider-Man is; a farewell to art teacher Miss Kramer; and breaking news that a salamander has escaped.
- Various Captain America educational videos were filmed but not used. These include Cap persuading students to not use illegal fireworks on the Fourth of July, Cap encouraging students to eat a balanced diet, Cap expounding the importance of math and reading, Cap teaching students about puberty, Cap hosting a video for students whose parents opted to not have their child participate in the health class on human reproduction, and Cap warning students about tooth decay and head lice.
- Two scenes were created—and can be seen in trailers—but never

intended to be a part of the film. The Vulture swooping down a hotel atrium was done for a sizzle reel shown at San Diego Comic-Con (the film was only a few weeks into production at that point). Spider-Man swinging next to Iron Man flying was made so that it could be included in the film's trailer. Originally, a shot from the Staten Island Ferry scene was to have been used as the background plate, but this was deemed not good enough, and so it was changed to Queens.

Location, Location

To catch viewers up, we see a home video of the events of *Captain America: Civil War* from Peter Parker's perspective. As part of this, we see him drive past the **Unisphere** of Flushing Meadows-Corona Park in New York on his way to the airport, drive down **Warschauer Straße** (close to where it intersects Kopernikusstraße) in Berlin, Germany, and visit the **Brandenburg Gate** (Pariser Platz, Berlin), before participating in the airport fight.

Unlike past Spider-Man films, *Homecoming* largely eschews the skyscrapers of Manhattan and instead has the web-slinger spend most of his time hanging around Queens. Scenes filmed in New York took place at various locations around the city, though the bulk of the production was completed in Atlanta, Georgia. **Peter Parker's apartment** can be found at 4325 43rd Street, Sunnyside, New York. While the film has audiences believe Peter alights at **36 Avenue station**, it's actually 75 St–Elderts Lane station that was used for filming. Over in Brooklyn, Franklin K Lane High School (999 Jamaica Avenue) serves as the exterior to **Midtown School of Science & Technology**, with the interiors being filmed at Henry W Grady High School (929 Charles Allen Drive NE) in Atlanta. Franklin K Lane is now closed, with several different schools sharing the campus. Also in Atlanta is **Delmar's Deli-Grocery** (92 Peachtree Street SW), the retail space dressed up to appear as such. On the diagonally opposite corner is the shop front that stood in for the fictional **Queens Community Bank** (97 Peachtree Street SW).

We then see Peter run across 31st Street and into an **alley** (between Stop-N-Go Astoria, Inc. at 2259 31st Street and Santander Bank at 2259 31st Street) where he strips down to his boxers before donning the Spidey suit. Though the street and alley entrance were filmed on location in New York, the alley itself is in Atlanta, and can be found next to Sidebar (79 Poplar Street NW). **Spidey subdues a bike thief** outside of Rainbow, a women's clothing store located at 62 Peachtree Street SW, Atlanta. While standing on the roof of Kings

Brandenburg Gate

Spirit of America

Fried Chicken (116-23 Jamaica Avenue, Richmond Hill, New York), **Spider-Man is asked to perform a flip** by a hot dog vendor below. The property where **Spider-Man stops who he thinks is a car thief** can be found at 4337 43rd Street, Sunnyside, which is next to the building used as Peter's apartment. Come sunset, **Spider-Man reports to Happy while perched on the fire escape** above Sunnysight Optik (44-13 Queens Boulevard, Sunnyside). One of the stores of the Sylvan Building, located at 233 Mitchell Street SW, Atlanta, is used as **Prachya Thai**.

Liz's house can be found at 229 Little John Trail NE, Atlanta. Skipping out on the party being held there, **Spider-Man goes to thwart the sale of illegal weapons**, with shooting having occurred underneath Park Drive Bridge (Park Drive NE, Atlanta). Having tethered himself to the van by a web line, **Spider-Man is flung into a bin** as the vehicle turns the bend on Lionel Lane NE in Atlanta. The **Indian wedding** Tony Stark attends was shot at the Hindu Temple of Atlanta (5851 Highway 85, Riverdale, Georgia).

As the kids head to the decathlon, their bus drives over the **Arlington Memorial Bridge**. Though we are told it's held in Washington DC, Atlanta's Embassy Suites by Hilton Atlanta Perimeter Center (1030 Crown Pointe Parkway) was in fact used as the site of the **United States Academic Decathlon**. For the **Damage Control warehouse**, production used the Georgia World Congress Center (285 Andrew Young International Boulevard NW, Atlanta). Rushing to get to his friends, **Spidey rides on top of a tour bus**. We first see the bus turn right from Washington DC's 23rd Street SW onto Lincoln Memorial Circle NW, only for the subsequent shot of the bus to show it back on 23rd Street SW heading north. The bus continues on Lincoln Memorial Circle NW, with Spider-Man jumping off as it approaches Daniel French Drive SW. As he continues to talk to Liz, Spider-Man runs down the length of the **Lincoln Memorial Reflecting Pool**. For the **Washington Monument**, the filmmakers built a thirty-foot (nine-metre) tall portion of the obelisk on an outdoor set in Atlanta. Indoor sets standing in for smaller sections of the Washington Monument were also used.

Part of the Staten Island Ferry sequence was filmed on the real *Spirit of America*, with a section of the vessel also being built on the backlot of Pinewood Atlanta Studios (461 Sandy Creek Road, Fayetteville, Georgia). The studio has since rebranded and is now called Trilith Studios. En route to the homecoming, Adrian Toomes drives Peter and Liz down New York's **Jamaica Avenue**, passing 118th Street. Behind the wheel of Flash's car, **Peter drives through the streets of New York**, though the sequence was filmed in Atlanta. We first see him turn right from Jesse Hill Jr Drive NE onto Auburn Avenue NE. The car is then filmed travelling east on Auburn Avenue NE going through the Fort Street NE intersection as Peter explains to Ned that he hasn't really driven before—in fact, we see Peter go through the intersection twice! With the car's headlights now turned on, the vehicle is filmed travelling north on Peachtree Center Avenue NE before turning right onto Auburn Avenue NE. The warehouse complex at 715-741 Ralph David Abernathy Boulevard SW in Atlanta was used as the **Vulture's lair**.

THOR: RAGNAROK

Director: Taika Waititi
Screenplay: Eric Pearson and Craig Kyle & Christopher L Yost

Producer: Kevin Feige
Executive Producers: Louis D'Esposito, Victoria Alonso, Brad Winderbaum, Thomas M Hammel, and Stan Lee
Co-Producer: David J Grant
Associate Producer: Brian Chapek

Cinematography: Javier Aguirresarobe
Production Design: Dan Hennah and Ra Vincent
Editing: Joel Negron and Zene Baker
Music: Mark Mothersbaugh
Costume Design: Mayes C Rubeo
Visual Effects Supervisor: Jake Morrison
Casting: Sarah Halley Finn

Production Company: Marvel Studios
Distribution Company: Walt Disney Studios Motion Pictures

US Release Date: 3 November 2017
Running Time: 130 minutes
Budget: $180 million
Box Office: $854,189,384

Based on the Marvel Comics by Stan Lee, Larry Lieber, and Jack Kirby

Cast: Chris Hemsworth (*Thor*), Tom Hiddleston (*Loki*), Cate Blanchett (*Hela*), Idris Elba (*Heimdall*), Jeff Goldblum (*Grandmaster*), Tessa Thompson (*Valkyrie*), Karl Urban (*Skurge*), Mark Ruffalo (*Bruce Banner/Hulk*), Anthony Hopkins (*Odin*), Benedict Cumberbatch (*Doctor Strange*), Taika Waititi (*Korg*), Rachel House (*Topaz*), Clancy Brown (*Surtur*), Tadanobu Asano (*Hogun*), Ray Stevenson (*Volstagg*), Zachary Levi (*Fandral*), Luke Hemsworth (*Actor Thor*), Sam Neill (*Actor Odin*), Charlotte Nicdao (*Actor Sif*), Shalom Brune-Franklin (*College Girl #1*), Taylor Hemsworth (*College Girl #2*), Steven Oliver (*Cousin Carlo*), Hamish Parkinson (*Beerbot 5000*), Shari Sebbens (*Asgardian Mother*), Matt Damon (*Actor Loki*), Stan Lee (*Barber*)

Thor finds himself trapped on Sakaar, where he is forced to take part in a gladiatorial contest. The God of Thunder must escape if he is to stop his sister, Hela, who has taken the throne, as well as prevent Ragnarok — the destruction of Asgard.

Though a financial success, *Thor: The Dark World*'s (2013) mixed critical reception suggested that the formula used for the first two *Thor* films needed to change. Alan Taylor indicated that he would not return due to his displeasure with the post-production process, which resulted in a film that didn't match his vision. Ruben Fleischer, Rob Letterman, and Rawson Marshall Thurber were in contention to replace him as director, though it would be New Zealand filmmaker Taika Waititi who won Marvel over with his pitch for the third instalment. A lighter tone would be employed, with humour used throughout—a big element in Waititi's previous films *Boy* (2010), *What We Do in the Shadows* (2014), and *Hunt for the Wilderpeople* (2016)—turning the once-serious fantasy series into a comedy. Waititi used classic '80s films *Flash Gordon* (1980) and *Big Trouble in Little China* (1986) as inspiration for the film's tone.

The change in direction for the franchise also meant changes to Thor's character. Chris Hemsworth loathed the wig he had to wear when portraying the character, and so the decision was made to shave the God of Thunder's head. Thor's Shakespearean dialogue and accent were reduced, with more humour injected into the character. It was reasoned this was a trait he picked up from Tony Stark from his time spent on Earth. Tom Hiddleston's Loki and Anthony Hopkins' Odin make a return, concluding a thread that had been set up in *The Dark World*. Asgardian gatekeeper Heimdall, played by Idris Elba, also makes an appearance.

Mark Ruffalo makes a return as fellow Avenger Bruce Banner/Hulk, with *Ragnarok* beginning a new arc for the character that would continue in the next two *Avengers* films. The character was last seen flying off in a Quinjet in *Avengers: Age of Ultron* (2015), with a line changed in the script to imply he was on Earth rather than found in the vicinity of Saturn. This was to downplay the idea that the studio would be adapting the "Planet Hulk" story, which they had no intention of doing at the time. As the story for the third *Thor* film was being developed, the notion of Thor heading into space was brought up, leading to the inclusion of the Hulk and the use of elements from the "Planet Hulk" arc.

Newcomers to the franchise include: Jeff Goldblum as the Grandmaster, the hedonistic ruler of Sakaar; Tessa Thompson as Valkyrie; Karl Urban as Skurge; and Waititi himself portraying Korg, basing his performance on Polynesian bouncers. Australian actress Cate Blanchett was the top choice for Hela, the Goddess of Death and Odin's forgotten daughter. Thus, *Raganarok* would be the first MCU film to have a lead female villain. Blanchett worked out for the physically demanding role, training in cardio and weights with Luke Zocchi, Hemsworth's personal trainer.

Principal photography on *Ragnarok* commenced on 4 July 2016, with filming taking place in the Australian state of Queensland, reflecting Hemsworth's wish for the production to film in his home country. Waititi's directorial style resulted in a very relaxed set, encouraging collaboration, with much of the film's dialogue improvised. Being of Māori descent, he was also instrumental in having Māori and Aboriginal Australians working on the film in departments such as stunts and set design, as well as hiring Indigenous Australian actors, such as Steven Oliver and Shari Sebbens.

After locating his father and meeting his older sister, a large part of the film finds Thor trapped on the planet Sakaar. Though not a location created by comic book artist Jack Kirby, the filmmakers used his distinct design aesthetic in bringing parts of the alien world to life. To this end, vibrant colours, geometric shapes, bold lines, and asymmetry were used in the design of the sets, ships, weapons, and costumes.

In spite of the fantastical nature of the project, costume designer Mayes Rubeo ensured physical costumes for the principal actors were created to give them a sense of how their characters would look and feel, even if they ended up wearing mocap suits on set. When we first see Thor, he's decked out in a very rugged outfit, a reflection of his long journey through space.

His Sakaaran gladiator look was designed as if it had been cobbled together from various parts, with his arms left largely exposed to make him more agile. Thor's helmet, meanwhile, was made to evoke the character's classic comic book helmet without being descendent from Asgard. The piece was produced by Weta Workshop who also manufactured sixteen Sakaaran guard suits, Skurge's costume, and a full-sized helmet and pauldron for the Hulk, which was used to aid the visual effects artists.

For the Grandmaster, his tunic was designed to have a loungewear aesthetic with geometric shapes. It's also asymmetric—linking it with the haphazard angles and shapes of Sakaar—with the use of gold symbolizing his high status. Unlike his comic book counterpart, the Grandmaster isn't depicted with blue skin in the film, with Waititi noting that Goldblum previously portrayed a blue-coloured character in *Earth Girls Are Easy* (1988) and that he didn't want the makeup to detract from the actor's performance. For Hela's outfit, Rubeo tried to be as faithful to the comic costume as possible, turning to Ironhead Studio to help produce it. While a physical version of Hela's headpiece was created via 3D printing, Blanchett didn't wear it throughout the shoot due to its size and weight. Instead the actress would don a mocap hat, with the helmet added in with CGI. The antlers of the physical helmet were modular, reflecting how the actual number of antlers would change throughout the film as Hela manipulates them.

On 10 October 2017, *Thor: Ragnarok* had its world premiere at the El Capitan Theatre in Los Angeles. Waititi's eclectic mix of humour, zany set designs, and self-referential nature turned out to be what the *Thor* franchise needed—a wonderful refresh after the first two more sombre instalments. Hemsworth made the God of Thunder's comedic turn seem natural, fans were presented with a more nuanced Hulk, and Blanchett was effortlessly menacing. With *Thor: Ragnarok*, audiences aren't so much given a third *Thor* film, but a fresh, distinct entry in the Marvel Cinematic Universe.

Excelsior!
Stan Lee cuts Thor's hair, telling him to be still as his hands aren't as steady as they used to be.

Mid-Credits Scene
Thor and Loki discuss their return to Earth, just as Thanos' ship, the *Sanctuary II*, looms in front of them.

Post-Credits Scene
The Grandmaster finds himself surrounded by many Sakaarians. He declares their revolution a success and points out that he played a big part in it since he's the figure they wanted to overthrow.

Marvellous Miscellanea
- The film's working title during production was *Creature Report*.
- Surtur's horns were created from a boomerang that was gifted to the film crew.
- It's surprising that Led Zeppelin's "Immigrant Song"—a song with references to Norse mythology—hadn't previously been used in a *Thor* film. Waititi included the track in his sizzle reel (which also contained clips from movies the director had illegally torrented) to convey to Marvel the tone he envisioned for the project. Kevin Feige was impressed with its use and so the song was carried over into the final film.
- The Shake Weight Skurge uses actually belongs to Waititi. The director bought it during his time working on the 2011 film *Green Lantern* (he played Thomas Kalmaku), having stayed up late one night and seeing the infomercial for it.
- Fellow New Zealand actor Sam Neill appears in the film as the actor who portrays Odin in Loki's play (Neill appeared in *Hunt for the Wilderpeople*). The actor portraying Thor in the play is Chris' older brother Luke Hemsworth, while Matt Damon—who's friends with Chris—appears as the actor playing Loki. Interestingly, Damon previously played a character named Loki in the 1999 film *Dogma*.
- Due to a scheduling conflict with her work on the television show *Blindspot* (2015-20), Jamie Alexander was unable to reprise her role as Sif, her absence cheekily acknowledged in Loki's play.
- This isn't the first time a place called Shady Acres (the name of the care home where Loki hides Odin) has appeared on screen. It originates from *Ace Ventura: Pet Detective* (1994), where it's a mental hospital, the name being a play on director Tom Shadyac's name. In *South Park* (1997-) it's the name of a retirement community.
- Taylor Hemsworth, Chris Hemsworth's second cousin, plays the college girl who tells Thor that she's sorry to hear Jane Foster dumped him.
- After Valkyrie asks to be paid ten million units in exchange for Thor, Topaz says to the Grandmaster, "Tell her she's dreamin'." This is a

reference to a much-used line from the Australian film *The Castle* (1997).
- The spaceships in the film are named after various Holden car models. These include the *Commodore* (the circular ship that serves as the Grandmaster's leisure vessel), the *Statesman* (the ship the Asgardian refugees board), *Escort*, *Kingswood*, and *Torana*. The exception to this is Valkyrie's which is called the *Warsong*, taken from a poem about the valkyries.
- The red, black, and yellow colouring of the *Commodore* is a reference to the Australian Aboriginal flag, while the red, black, and white design of the *Warsong* reflects the Māori (Tino Rangatiratanga) flag.
- In addition to directing the film and portraying Korg, Waititi did the motion capture for Surtur and appears as one of Harjo's heads (he's the left one). Stunt performer Shane Rangi is the middle head (according to Rangi, the original plan was to have him portray all three heads), while the right head is Chris Hemsworth. Harjo is named after Waititi's friend Sterlin Harjo.
- Valkyrie opening a bottle of beer with a dagger pays homage to *Once Were Warriors* (1994), in which Beth Heke opens bottles of beer using a spatula/fish slice in a similar manner.
- Look closely and you'll see the letter 'N' shaved into one side of Thor's head, with the other bearing the letter 'Z', referring to New Zealand.
- The line "He's a friend from work" was a suggestion given to Chris Hemsworth by a kid who visited the set as part of the Make-A-Wish Foundation.
- Hemsworth's wife, Elsa Pataky, plays one of the nurses tending to Thor after his fight with the Hulk while another nurse is played by Waititi's wife, Chelsea Winstanley.
- The Valkyrie flashback sequence was filmed using a lighting rig invented by Carlo van de Roer and Stu Rutherford, who both attended high school with Waititi. Dubbed DynamicLight, the rig comprises of a circular array of 200 lights, with each light flashing one after another in less than a second, with the result being captured by high-speed cameras. *Ragnarok* was the first film to use the technology.
- Indigenous Australians who interned on set made many of the Hulk-themed banners and masks seen during the parade on Sakaar.
- There's a subtle rock-paper-scissors joke that runs throughout the film. It's revealed by Korg himself that he was sent to Sakaar as punishment for trying to start a revolution. His plan failed as a result of him not

handing out enough pamphlets (paper beating rock). Towards the end of the movie, Korg thinks he's killed his friend Miek (rock beating scissors).
- The film was called *Mighty Thor: Battle Royale* in Japan, with "Ragnarok" being an unfamiliar word in the country.

From Panels to the Screen

Ragnarok in the Marvel Universe is very much like the Ragnarök of Norse mythology, essentially a cycle of life and death. In the comics, it involves the destruction of Asgard and the deaths of many Asgardians. They are then reborn after some time, and the cycle starts all over again. The Ragnarok story the film mostly draws from spans *Thor* #80-85 (2004), aptly titled "Ragnarok." During a mission to find out if Ragnarok can be stopped, Thor discovers that a group of gods known as Those Who Sit Above in Shadow consume the energy released from Ragnarok, and thus keep the cycle going. He resolves to end the cycle of Ragnarok by having it occur one last time. Thor proceeds to destroy the Loom of the Fates, severing Asgard's tie to Those Who Sit Above in Shadow. Of note, Thor's hammer, Mjolnir, was destroyed in *Thor* #80 (though this is not the first time it has been damaged). Also, in *Thor* #85, Thor asks Surtur to reforge Mjolnir, and in exchange Thor allows the Fire Demon and his forces to travel to Asgard unhindered to wreak destruction.

While this may be the third *Thor* film, it also adapts the "Planet Hulk" storyline (*The Incredible Hulk* #92-105, 2006-07, *Giant-Size Hulk* #1, 2006). The Hulk is sent into space by the Illuminati, the group believing that he is too dangerous to remain on Earth. Instead of landing on a planet without sentient life as intended, the Hulk's shuttle goes off course and crashes on Sakaar where he's enslaved and forced to fight in gladiatorial battles for the Red King. It is from this story that the film adapts Hulk's gladiator costume, while his beaded necklaces and skirt are taken from *Ultimate Wolverine vs. Hulk* #1-6 (2005-09), where he spent time at a Tibetan monastery.

In the comics, Surtur is a massive Fire Demon and ruler of Muspelheim. He possesses immense strength, can produce flames, and wields a sword called Twilight. The comic book incarnation of Skurge is a half-Storm-Giant, half-Asgardian warrior who earned the moniker "the Executioner" after slaying many Storm Giants in battle. His double-bladed axe allowed him to open dimensional rifts and produce blasts of ice and fire. Skurge aiding Hela in the film is similar to how he often helped the Enchantress with her schemes (albeit, manipulated into doing so). The MCU version of Skurge dying while fighting on the side of good is similar to his demise in the comics. In *Thor* #362 (1985), Skurge dies while holding the bridge of Gjallerbru (using automatic rifles!) against the creatures of Hel, allowing Thor and his companions to escape.

In the film, the stage-Loki apologises to stage-Thor for the time he turned him into a frog. Thor has indeed transformed into the amphibious creature in the source material, occurring in *Thor* #363 (1986). After the play, Thor threatens Loki with Mjolnir, which will return to his hand whilst he holds the trickster god's neck. This is taken from *Thor* #359 (1985). In the issue, Thor uses the tactic to force Loki to free him from a love spell that was placed on him.

Thor, in his civilian guise, banging his "umbrella" down to reveal his Asgardian garb is a nod to how Donald Blake would strike down a stick (a disguised Mjolnir) to transform into the God of Thunder. During the final battle, Thor loses an eye to Hela. A one-eyed Thor does exist in the comics—the Thor of Earth-14412, who is king of Asgard.

In the comics, Hela is the Goddess of Death and ruler of Hel and Niffleheim. She is the daughter of Loki and Angrboda—a detail understandably not carried over into the Marvel Cinematic Universe. Thor having a sister, however, does have precedence in the source material, though it is Angela who is the thunder god's sibling, not Hela. Hela's powers in the comic books include enhanced strength, energy projection, teleportation, illusion casting, levitation, and the ability to kill Asgardians when in contact with their skin. She becomes weakened if her cloak is ever removed, and her true form is revealed, the left side of her face appearing decayed. Hela's ability to manifest weapons in the movie is a power afforded to wielders of a weapon known as All-Black, of whom the most well-known is Gorr the God Butcher. In fact, Hela's line "What are you the god of?" is taken from Gorr—a question he poses to Thor in *Thor: God of Thunder* #2 (2012).

In the source material, Brunnhilde/Valkyrie is an Asgardian warrior and leader of the Valkyrior, a group tasked by Odin to bring the slain worthy heroes to Valhalla. She wields a virtually indestructible sword called Dragonfang and rides winged horses. The comic book version of the character has blonde hair (there is a nod to this in the film with a blonde-haired Valkyrie saving Scrapper 142), while the cinematic incarnation has black hair. The MCU Valkyrie's moniker, Scrapper 142, is a reference to *The Incredible Hulk* #142 (1971), the first appearance of Samantha Parrington as Valkyrie. A reality-hopping Valkyrie bearing a resemblance to Tessa Thompson's incarnation was introduced into the comics, making her debut in *Exiles* #2 (2018).

The comic book incarnation of En Dwi Gast/the Grandmaster is an Elder of the Universe who has a penchant for playing and collecting games. He possesses a vast intellect and, like his fellow Elders, doesn't age, being virtually immortal. In the film, the Grandmaster has a blue marking running from his bottom lip down to his chin. This is a nod to the character's blue skin in the comics. The marking is also seen on the cinematic version of the Collector, a possible nod to how they see each other as brothers in the source material, due to them being the last of their respective species (as is the case with the other Elders of the Universe). The Grandmaster refers to his gladiatorial battles as the "Contest of Champions," referencing the limited series of the same name (*Marvel Super Hero Contest of Champions* #1-3, 1982). The story sees the Grandmaster challenging Death for the chance to resurrect the Collector, with both sides using heroes from Earth as pawns.

Adorning the Grandmaster's tower on Sakaar are head sculptures of Man-Thing (guardian of the Nexus of All Realities), Beta Ray Bill (a Korbinite warrior who wields the hammer Stormbreaker), Ares (Olympian god of war), Dark-Crawler (an extradimensional warrior who wields the Sceptre of Shadow), and Bi-Beast (an android with two heads, one on top of each other).

In both media, Korg is a Kronan who was enslaved on Sakaar. In the comics, however, he arrives on Sakaar after his ship crash-lands on the planet while trying to get back home. He became a member of the Warbound, a group led by the Hulk that started a rebellion and overthrew the Red King. Miek is also a member of the Warbound. The comic book incarnation belongs to the insectivorid race called Natives. Unlike his cinematic counterpart, the comic book version can actually speak.

Bruce Banner's analogy of how last time the Hulk was in control he felt as though the Hulk "had the keys to the car [while he] was locked in the trunk" is lifted from *The Totally Awesome Hulk* #1 (2015), which features Amadeus Cho as the Green Goliath. In the film, Thor leads a group called the Revengers, comprising of Valkyrie, Bruce Banner, and Loki. Various teams calling themselves the Revengers exist within the Marvel Multiverse. Led by Wonder Man, the Earth-616 incarnation of the group attacked the Avengers, believing that the superhero team does far more damage to the world than they do helping it.

The comic book incarnation of Fenris Wolf (simply referred to as Fenris in the film) is a large wolf with the ability to change its form into that of a wolf-like humanoid. Though he isn't Hela's pet in the comics, she did enlist his help to bring about Ragnarok in *Thor* #277 (1978).

It's no secret that the art of Jack Kirby influenced the film's aesthetic. Many costumes borrow from the design of the Celestials. The wall art in the Grandmaster's booth is made up of classic Kirby art, with one portion being a re-coloured version of a piece of technology that Kirby drew for *Fantastic Four* #64 (1967). And later on when Thor, Bruce Banner, and Valkyrie head towards the Devil's Anus, a green spaceship bearing a resemblance to a Celestial spaceship can be spotted (first seen in *The Eternals* #1, 1976, but a better look at it appears in the subsequent issue).

In the mid-credits scene, we see the *Sanctuary II*, a starship Thanos owns in the comics.

MCU Easter Eggs

While trapped in a cage on Muspelheim, Thor mentions that he fought some robots, which he did in *Avengers: Age of Ultron*. The play recounts Loki's "death" from *Thor: The Dark World*. Thor turns to Doctor Strange to help him track down Odin. The various objects housed in Odin's vault are seen once again such as the Infinity Gauntlet (which Hela points out is fake), the Casket of Ancient Winters (previously seen in 2011's *Thor*), the Tesseract, and the Eternal Flame. Loki points out that he's Thor's adopted brother, much like how Thor pointed out that Loki was adopted in *The Avengers* (2012). Thor attempts to use Black Widow's lullaby to calm the Hulk. Another callback to *The Avengers* is when Hulk thrashes Thor, doing so in a similar manner to when he thrashed Loki. The password Thor has to use to activate the Quinjet is "Point Break" (Tony Stark's nickname for him in *The Avengers*). Valkyrie suggests going to Asgard via Xandar, the latter being a planet first seen in *Guardians of the Galaxy* (2014). Bruce Banner attempts to turn into the Hulk by falling from a height (as he did in the 2008 film *The Incredible Hulk*).

Chopped, Changed, and Lengthened

- In a draft of the script, an alternate ending for Loki was conceived. Instead of remaining on board the *Statesman* with Thor and the other Asgardians, Loki would have snuck off, his whereabouts revealed in *Avengers: Infinity War*.
- An alternate ending to Thor's conversation with Doctor Strange sees the latter conjure a map identifying Odin's location using a strand of Thor's

- hair. Strange also produces a key (which Thor spits out from his mouth), which we soon find unlocks Loki from the portable toilet he's trapped in.
- Thor and Loki locate Odin in an alley. He's currently living as a homeless person. Thor tries to take his father back to Asgard, but Odin tells his son that Asgard is not a place and warns him about Ragnarok and the reappearance of Hela. Hela then appears and kills Odin. Thor throws his hammer at her, but she catches it and breaks it. Loki calls to Skurge to bring him and Thor back to Asgard via the Bifrost. This version wasn't used, as Waititi wanted Odin and his sons to connect emotionally before his death, feeling the New York alley wasn't a location suited for this. The scene featured the words "Skux Life" as graffiti in the background, a nod to *Hunt for the Wilderpeople* in which the character Ricky Baker says, "I didn't choose the skux life, the skux life chose me."
- According to Zachary Levi, after Hela throws her blades into Fandral, he said "For Asgard" as he died, but the line ended up being cut from the film.
- Skurge—surrounded by the remnants of Hela's battle with Asgardian warriors—spots Heimdall escaping through the city with Asgardian citizens. Heimdall, noticing he's being watched, looks back at Skurge.
- An extended version of Thor meeting the Grandmaster sees the latter ordering his guards to shoot the small flying creatures that have flown into the room before explaining the obedience disks to a restrained Thor. Thor introduces himself as the God of Thunder before Topaz comes past and informs the Grandmaster that his cousin, Carlo, has been found. Cutting to the next scene, we see Carlo restrained in a chair like Thor. Carlo admits that he's been gambling (Thor and the Grandmaster have trouble understanding him, initially mishearing his confession as "scambling" and "camping") and the Grandmaster "pardons" him, using a melting stick to kill him.
- As Thor is being dragged away to get his hair cut, Korg wishes him luck. He then admits to Miek that he doesn't think Thor will be able to defeat the Grandmaster's champion, which Thor overhears.
- Thor is in Hulk's chambers and is tugging on his obedience disk in an effort to take it off. Hulk is moving and talking in his sleep as if in a fight. Waking up, he talks to Thor, but they end up arguing with Thor saying that the Hulk is the "stupid Avenger" while Hulk claims that Thor is the "tiny Avenger."

- A scene was shot in which Valkyrie's bisexuality would have been implied, with a woman seen walking out of her bedroom. The sequence was cut as it was felt it distracted from the exposition that was being delivered.
- Thor crashes through the window of Hulk's room on Sakaar. He slides down the building, leaping to another, sliding down that, and making his way to the streets below. Thor then walks through a market area when the Hulk lands behind him. People are cheering when he does and the Hulk embraces this. He sees Thor running and begins to chase after him. Thor eventually makes it to the junkyard where the Quinjet is held.
- The Grandmaster motions for Loki and Valkyrie to find Thor and Hulk, but both are unable to interpret his hand gesture until he explains it. After they leave, he talks to Topaz about universal signs. He does a motion with his hands which she incorrectly identifies as dialling it down, get out, smaller, wanting dessert, and paying the bill, before the Grandmaster gives up and explains that he's asking for the cheque.
- According to Waititi, a scene was shot in which Korg, having been set free by Valkyrie, is trying to start his revolution. He and other freed gladiators are in the weapons vault choosing weapons, but it isn't going well, with Korg clueless as to how to run a revolution.
- The Grandmaster is travelling in an aircraft in pursuit of Thor, Bruce, and Valkyrie as they head towards the Devil's Anus. He locks onto their vehicle, but Bruce flies up to avoid the blasts, resulting in the Grandmaster flying past them and crashing into a ship ahead.
- As they approach the Devil's Anus, Thor and Bruce congratulate each other on their actions in eluding the pursuing Sakaarians. Bruce voices his concern that he'll turn into the Hulk upon entering the wormhole and not being able to revert back. Getting closer to the wormhole, Bruce has Thor strap him into a seat.
- On board the Grandmaster's ship, Thor (who was watching a hologram of the Grandmaster being caressed by tentacles) has a conversation with Bruce, discussing the deaths of their fathers, with Thor pondering whether or not he can defeat his sister, Hela, without his hammer. During this, Bruce eats what he believes to be some noodles, which turn out to be the tail of an alien creature.
- Several shots used in the film's trailers don't appear in the final version, such as Loki flipping two knives, Thor still having two eyes when

fighting on the Bifrost (done to preserve the fact that he loses one), and Loki, Valkyrie, Thor, and the Hulk standing next to each other ready to confront Hela.

Location, Location

Filming of *Thor: Ragnarok* was based at Village Roadshow Studios (Entertainment Road, Oxenford) in Queensland, Australia. All nine sound stages were utilised (the **Grandmaster's palace** was built on the largest: the 3,716-square-metre Stage 9), as well as the backlot where sets for **Asgard's piazza** and the **streets of Sakaar** were constructed. **Muspelheim's rocky exterior** was based on the topography of Dirk Hartog Island, located off the coast of Western Australia.

Esk Lane

An empty lot on the corner of Margaret Street and Albert Street in Brisbane was used as the location for the demolished **Shady Acres Care Home**. Thor and Loki track Odin to a **Norwegian field**, which was shot in Atlanta, Georgia. Port Talbot in Wales and Norway's Lofoten Islands were used as reference for the surrounding landscape. Originally, Hela destroys Mjolnir in an **alley**, the scene being filmed in Brisbane's Esk Lane. At the time of writing, Esk Lane is being converted to an underground train station to be called Albert Street station. The **Sakaaran junkyard** was filmed at Oxenford Quarry (33 Maudsland Road, Oxenford). The **Asgardian forest** through which Heimdall leads a group of refugees was filmed at Queensland's Tamborine National Park, with the waterfall he comes across being Cedar Creek Falls.

BLACK PANTHER

Director: Ryan Coogler
Screenplay: Ryan Coogler & Joe Robert Cole

Producer: Kevin Feige
Executive Producers: Louis D'Esposito, Victoria Alonso, Nate Moore, Jeffrey Chernov, and Stan Lee
Co-Producer: David J Grant

Cinematography: Rachel Morrison
Production Design: Hannah Beachler
Editing: Michael P Shawver and Debbie Berman
Music: Ludwig Göransson
Costume Design: Ruth Carter
Visual Effects Supervisor: Geoffrey Baumann
Casting: Sarah Halley Finn

Production Company: Marvel Studios
Distribution Company: Walt Disney Studios Motion Pictures

US Release Date: 16 February 2018
Running Time: 134 minutes
Budget: $200 million
Box Office: $1,347,597,973

Based on the Marvel Comics by Stan Lee and Jack Kirby

Cast: Chadwick Boseman (*T'Challa/Black Panther*), Michael B Jordan (*Erik Killmonger*), Lupita Nyong'o (*Nakia*), Danai Gurira (*Okoye*), Martin Freeman (*Everett K Ross*), Daniel Kaluuya (*W'Kabi*), Letitia Wright (*Shuri*), Winston Duke (*M'Baku*), Sterling K Brown (*N'Jobu*), Angela Bassett (*Ramonda*), Forest Whitaker (*Zuri*), Andy Serkis (*Ulysses Klaue*), Florence Kasumba (*Ayo*), John Kani (*T'Chaka*), David S Lee (*Limbani*), Nabiyah Be (*Linda*), Isaach De Bankolé (*River Tribe Elder*), Connie Chiume (*Mining Tribe Elder*), Dorothy Steel (*Merchant Tribe Elder*), Danny Sapani (*Border Tribe Elder*), Stan Lee (*Thirsty Gambler*), Atandwa Kani (*Young T'Chaka*), Ashton Tyler (*Young T'Challa*), Denzel Whitaker (*James/Young Zuri*), Lucy Hockings (*BBC Reporter*), Seth Carr (*Young Killmonger*), Trevor Noah (*Griot*), Sebastian Stan (*Bucky Barnes/Winter Soldier*)

Following the death of his father, T'Challa returns to the African nation of Wakanda where he is crowned as the new king. His position is quickly challenged when a figure connected to his father's past emerges.

Black Panther: protector, warrior, and king. Not only is he Marvel's first superhero of African descent, he's also the first for mainstream American comics. It was about time the character featured in his own film. Wesley Snipes tried to get one made during the '90s, but it never eventuated. In October 2014, *Black Panther* was revealed to be a part of Phase Three, with a release date of 3 November 2017. It would later be pushed back to 6 July 2018 before settling on 16 February 2018.

Ava DuVernay was considered to direct, but eventually passed on the project, not wanting to compromise her vision despite seeing the cultural impact the film could have. F Gary Gray was subsequently sought after, but chose to direct *The Fate of the Furious* (2017) instead. Ryan Coogler would be announced as the director in January 2016. Coogler was familiar with Black Panther having discovered the character as a kid. He had been courted for several months, but at one point the negotiations stagnated. The critical acclaim of *Creed* (2015), however, saw them recommence. A graduate of the USC School of Cinematic Arts, Coogler came to prominence with his first feature film, *Fruitvale Station* (2013), which won the Grand Jury Prize and Audience Award for a dramatic film at the 2013 Sundance Film Festival.

To Coogler, *Black Panther* would deal with issues of identity and black culture. To that end the director ensured Wakanda was rooted in reality, even though it was a technologically advanced nation. Coogler went to Africa for research, visiting the countries of Kenya, Lesotho, and South Africa. Characters would also speak Xhosa (an official language of South Africa and Zimbabwe), while the Jabari tribe would speak Igbo (a native language of Nigeria), which represents the tribe's separateness from others in Wakanda.

Chadwick Boseman returns as T'Challa/Black Panther, with many other black actors cast in major roles. Lupita Nyong'o was cast as Nakia, a Wakandan spy and T'Challa's former lover. The Academy-Award-winning actress learnt how to speak Hausa and trained in judo and silat to prepare for the part. The role of Okoye, head of the Dora Milaje, went to Danai Gurira, with Coogler having her in mind after seeing her in *Mother of George* (2013). Letitia Wright and Angela Bassett were cast as Shuri and Ramonda respectively. W'Kabi—T'Challa's best friend—would be played by Daniel Kaluuya; Forest Whitaker was cast as Zuri, Wakanda's spiritual leader; and Winston Duke was cast as M'Baku, leader of the Jabari tribe.

A comic book reader in his youth, Michael B Jordon—who previously appeared as the Human Torch in *Fantastic Four* (2015)—would play Erik Killmonger. The role sees Jordan reunite with Coogler, having appeared in his previous two films. To prepare, the actor listened to speeches by Fred Hampton, Huey P Newton, Malcolm X, and Marcus Garvey. Jordon also got into a lonely mindset, isolating himself and shutting himself off from emotions such as love, for which he needed therapy to help him get out of after filming wrapped. Andy Serkis and Martin Freeman reprise their respective roles as Ulysses Klaue and Everett K Ross, with both characters making their second appearance in the MCU.

Black Panther began filming in January 2017. Production was based in Atlanta, Georgia, with second unit filming a car chase in South Korea, and plates shot in South Africa, Uganda, and Zambia.

Michael B Jordon wouldn't be the only past collaborator Coogler would bring onto *Black Panther*. The director reteamed with production designer Hannah Beachler and composer Ludwig Göransson—who both worked on his past two movies—and *Fruitvale Station* cinematographer, Rachel Morrison. This ensured Coogler's sensibility would be translated across many facets of production.

As a starting point, Hannah Beachler turned to the source material—with aid from her nineteen-year-old son, Dominic—researching Black Panther and his world. Other inspiration came from African architecture, the works of

Zaha Hadid, as well as a trip to South Africa and Lesotho. From this, Beachler compiled a 515-page guide containing the history of Wakanda to inform the set designs. The Warrior Falls were constructed in Atlanta, with a thirty-foot (nine-metre) high cliff face and a six-foot (1.8-metre) deep pool built above ground level. Visual effects would later be used to augment its size. Inspired by the Oribi Gorge, the cliffs were carved from styrofoam and covered with a layer of plaster, taking four months to construct. Tunnels were built into the back of the set, allowing extras to access and populate the cliff's many tiers. Additionally, a waterfall was added to the cliff edge via six large pumps that generated 30,000 gallons of water per minute. The past and present collide in the design of the tribal council room. Lots of circular shapes were used, a representation of the cyclical nature of life. During meetings, the tribe elders sit upon the flat top of a ruin, with glass and steel protecting the rest of the structure and forming the floor.

For the movie's many costumes, designer Ruth E Carter looked not just to the comics but to African culture and specific works by contemporary fashion designers Donna Karan, Yves Saint Laurent, and Issey Miyake. T'Challa's traditional robes are based off Nigerian senator suits. His tailcoat has dashiki-inspired embroidery and he wears sandals that are emblematic of Africa (which are actually modified Alexander McQueen shoes). All of this is to communicate his elegance and regality. Tribes are colour-coded and their dress based on specific African groups: the Border Tribe are dressed in blue, their clothes based on those worn by Lesotho shepherds; the River Tribe are dressed in green, their clothes based on those worn by the Wagenia fisherman in the Democratic Republic of Congo as well as the Suri and Tsamai tribes; the Merchant Tribe are dressed in purple, their clothes based on those worn by the Tuareg people; the Mining Tribe are dressed in red and orange colours, their clothes based on those worn by the Dinka and Samburu tribes; and the Jabari Tribe are dressed in brown and white, their clothes based on those worn by the Ethiopian Karo tribe and Malian Dogon tribe. Colour coordination also extended to specific characters. Zuri's outfits are purple, signifying his high rank and connection with royalty. His shaman costume takes queues from clothing worn by Nigerian men, with the triangular pattern on his sleeves stemming from the Tuareg people. The Dora Milaje are decked out in red, with pieces of armour (meant to be vibranium) intended to look like jewellery—their neck and arm rings are inspired by the South African Ndebele people—while the beadwork takes inspiration from the Turkana people from northwest Kenya. Okoye, however, wears gold armour, a symbol of her status as leader of the Dora Milaje.

The world premiere of *Black Panther* was held at the Dolby Theatre in Hollywood on 29 January 2018. To say *Black Panther* was well received is an understatement. By the end of its run, it was the highest-grossing film by a black director, the highest grossing film domestically of 2018, and became the ninth highest grossing film of all time with a haul of over $1.3 billion. The lavish sets and ornate costumes with their many African influences bring Wakanda to life and present a rich, immersive experience for the senses. Even the film's score with its use of African instruments, and the modern soundtrack curated by Kendrick Lamar, furthers the idea of tradition colliding with the ever-changing present.

The efforts of Ryan Coogler, the cast, and the crew were greatly rewarded when *Black Panther* was nominated for a Best Picture Oscar—the first superhero film to do so. The movie also garnered six other nominations, going on to win Best Original Score, Best Costume Design, and Best Production Design at the 91st Academy Awards. *Black Panther* also garnered two wins at the 25th Annual Screen Actors Guild Awards, claiming the prize for Outstanding Performance by a Cast in a Motion Picture as well as Outstanding Performance by a Stunt Ensemble in a Motion Picture. Not only has the future of the Marvel Cinematic Universe changed, but also the landscape of Hollywood films in general.

Excelsior!
Stan Lee can be seen at the casino, claiming the chips T'Challa leaves behind.

Mid-Credits Scene
T'Challa appears before the UN, announcing that Wakanda will now open themselves up to the rest of the world.

Post-Credits Scene
Shuri checks up on Bucky and tells him there's more he needs to learn. According to Sebastian Stan, the scene was originally longer and included Bucky interacting with the Wakandans in the village.

Marvellous Miscellanea
- The working title for the film was *Motherland*.

- To help bring an authenticity to the score, composer Ludwig Göransson and his future wife, Serena McKinney, travelled around Africa and met with local musicians. In Senegal, he spent time with singer Baaba Maal as he was touring and also met up with Fula flute player Amadou Ba. In South Africa, he visited the International Library of African Music where he listened to various recordings of African tribes.
- The typeface used to depict the English words in the intertitles and the main-on-end title sequence is BEYNO, which was designed by Fabian Korn. It was production designer Hannah Beachler and graphic designer Zachary Fannin, however, who created the Wakandan script that's used throughout the film. There are in fact two versions: Modern Wakandan and Ancient Wakandan. A range of African scripts inspired the letterforms of Modern Wakandan including Bamum and Tifinagh, while Nsibidi was used as the basis for Ancient Wakandan.
- Killmonger grows up in Oakland, California, which is where director Ryan Coogler was born and spent his early childhood.
- As T'Challa, Okoye, and Nakia fly into Wakanda, the track "Wakanda" can be heard. It begins with Baaba Maal singing in Fula about an elephant that's just died, representative of T'Chaka's passing.
- The pose of pharaohs in ancient Egyptian statues as well as West African sculptures served as the inspiration for the Wakandan salute. The action also means "love" and "hug" in American Sign Language.
- The face paint patterns sported by Papua New Guinean shamans and warriors inspired Zuri's face paint design.
- Coogler used the debating scenes in the House of Representatives from *Lincoln* (2012) as inspiration for when M'Baku challenges T'Challa at Warrior Falls, having him use political messages to attack him.
- To shoot the scene of W'Kabi feeding an apple to his rhino, actor Daniel Kaluuya actually fed a horse, with the animal later replaced using CGI.
- The Wakandan words on the throne read "WISDOM" and "LOYALTY." The Wakanda text seen on T'Challa's right "sneaker" says "heir," while the left one has the name "tchaka." Additionally, when T'Challa strikes his new suit to test its kinetic energy absorption capabilities, look closely and you'll see that some of the glowing areas are actually Wakandan letters. When translated, one string of text reads "I Love You Mom," while next to it are the words "Fight for your—," which is incomplete.
- The colours of the Pan-African flag can be seen as the Wakandans arrive

at the illegal casino. T'Challa is dressed in a black suit, Nakia is wearing a green dress, while Okoye's dress is red.
- Attentive viewers may notice that fish scales decorate one of the casino walls, carved carp appear on stair posts, and carp adorn the casino chips. According to Beachler, these are a reference to a Korean folktale. In the story, a man catches a carp but decides to let it go. It turns out the carp is Yongwang, the Dragon King (in some versions it's Yongwang's son or grandson), and in turn the man is rewarded for his kind gesture.
- It took makeup designer Joel Harlow and a team of three other makeup artists roughly two-and-a-half to three-and-a-half hours each time to apply the approximately 3,000 prosthetic scars to Michael B Jordan.
- The handwriting seen in N'Jobu's diary belongs to production designer Hannah Beachler.
- As Killmonger oversees the burning of the heart-shaped herbs, two panther statues can be seen, foreshadowing T'Challa's survival.
- South African comedian Trevor Noah voices Griot, the artificial intelligence created by Shuri.

From Panels to the Screen

Located in Africa, Wakanda (officially the Kingdom of Wakanda) is a scientifically advanced country that, for most of its history, has isolated itself from the rest of the world. In the source material, it is composed of eighteen tribes whereas the film has reduced this number to five. The nation is notable for being a rich source of vibranium, thanks to a meteorite that crashed in the country. In the comics, the metal is sourced from the Great Mound, referred to on-screen as Mount Bashenga (Bashenga being one of the earliest Black Panthers in the comic books). Other notable Wakandan locations from the comics include Golden City (Wakanda's capital; also known as Birnin Zana in the source material) and Warrior Falls (where Killmonger fought T'Challa in ritual combat for the leadership of Wakanda in *Black Panther* #20, 2000).

In both media, while the Black Panther mantle is a hereditary title, one must pass several trials before taking on the role, and any Wakandan can attempt to challenge for the position. As part of these ordeals, the comic book incarnation of T'Challa had to defeat six warriors as well as the ruling Black Panther.

The Black Panther wears a black suit (in honour of the panther god Bast) with vibranium woven into it. The uniform T'Challa wears in the source material can absorb kinetic energy, has cloaking capabilities, and contains retractable claws. We see several versions of the Black Panther suit in the film, all of which appear to be interpretations of the various costumes T'Challa has worn in the comics. The Black Panther outfit with a gold chain could be based on the one from Christopher Priest's run (*Black Panther* #1-56, #59-62, 1998-2003). It is during this run that we learn the soles of the Black Panther costume have a vibranium alloy in them, allowing the wearer to effectively move without making a sound. T'Challa's new suit designed by Shuri was inspired by the one the character dons during Ta-Nehisi Coates' run (which began with *Black Panther* #1, 2016), in which the purple energy lines and retractable cowl are distinct features.

When T'Challa undergoes the ritual in which he ingests the heart-shaped herb, he visits the Ancestral Plane, where the spirits of previous Black Panthers reside. This appears to be a version of Djalia, a mystical realm that contains the history of Wakanda. Also taken from the comics are the Talon Fighters (the aircraft T'Challa travels in) and Kimoyo beads (which allow Wakandans to access the country's intranet).

The comic book incarnation of Nakia was romantically interested in T'Challa, though they were never in a relationship. The Marvel Cinematic Universe version of Nakia is a War Dog. This appears to be an adaptation of the Hatut Zeraze, or Dogs of War, Wakanda's secret police. Both the War Dogs and the Hatut Zeraze deal in espionage for the defence of Wakanda. Additionally, while the film depicts her as a spy, in the comics Nakia was a member of the Dora Milaje (being T'Challa's personal aide). She wears their uniform during the final battle in the film, which is most likely a nod to this fact. Other Dora Milaje with comic book counterparts include Okoye (in the source material she also acts as T'Challa's chauffeur) and Ayo (who previously appeared in *Captain America: Civil War*).

While the film depicts Ramonda as T'Challa's mother, in the comics she is specifically his stepmother. T'Challa's biological mother, N'Yami, died whilst giving birth to him. Following on from this, the comic book incarnation of Shuri is T'Challa's half-sister. While it appeared as if Shuri was going to challenge T'Challa for the throne, in the source material the character did actually become the Black Panther, doing so in *Black Panther* #5 (2009).

As seen in the film, the comic book version of Zuri is a friend of T'Chaka, though he is more of a warrior than a spiritual figure. In both the film and the comics, W'Kabi is the head of Wakandan security and a friend of T'Challa.

W'Kabi mentions that Ulysses Klaue was responsible for the death of his parents. This appears to be an incident taken from T'Challa's comic book past and transferred to W'Kabi.

In both media, M'Baku and his tribe, the Jabari, are not happy with T'Challa as Wakanda's ruler. While we don't see him wear a white gorilla costume, M'Baku does don a gorilla mask when challenging T'Challa, a nod to his Man-Ape persona in the comic books. Additionally, in the source material the Jabari tribe worships the gorilla god Ghekre whereas in the film they worship Hanuman (who, it must be noted, is a Hindu deity).

While T'Chaka had a brother in the comics, his brother was named S'Yan, not N'Jobu. In turn, S'Yan's son is named T'Shan, making him T'Challa's cousin. T'Challa's cousin in the film is Killmonger, whereas the comic book incarnation of Killmonger bears no familial relationship to him. In the film, we learn from N'Jobu that he and T'Chaka are the sons of Azzuri. Azzuri's comic book incarnation was the reigning Black Panther during WWII and father to T'Chaka and S'Yan.

In the comics, Erik Killmonger (born N'Jadaka; the film changes his real name to Erik Stevens, treating Killmonger as a nickname) grew up in Harlem, New York, having been captured by Ulysses Klaw. He would later return to his native Wakanda in an attempt to usurp T'Challa as ruler. Though he failed in his first attempt, Killmonger later succeeded in his goal, becoming chieftain of the Panther Clan in *Black Panther* #21 (2000). He later consumed the heart-shaped herb (doing so in *Black Panther* #24, 2000), but, as he was not of royal blood, fell into a coma. The tribal mask Erik dons while freeing Ulysses Klaue is reminiscent of the one the character wears in *Black Panther* #37-38 (2008), while the gold-spotted Black Panther suit he wears is a nod to the character's leopard, Preyy. Erik throwing T'Challa over Warrior Falls is taken from the end of *Jungle Action* #6 (1973).

Ulysses Klaue's mechanical hand is a reference to the character's use of a prosthetic sonic converter in place of his missing limb in the comics. The device could create solid sound structures as well as absorb and project sound waves. In fact, the comic book incarnation of Ulysses Klaw used a sound converter he created to transform his entire body to solidified sound, granting him enhanced strength and the ability to change his size.

When Black Panther apprehends Klaue in South Korea, the Wakandan king tells him, "Every breath you take is mercy from me." The line is taken from *New Avengers* #22 (2014), though in the issue the line is directed at

Namor. During the final battle, T'Challa fights a rhino, something the character did in the opening pages of *Jungle Action* #9 (1974). At the end of the film, some Wakandan boys refer to Bucky Barnes as "White Wolf." In the comics, White Wolf is the alias of Hunter, the leader of the Hatut Zeraze and T'Challa's adoptive brother.

MCU Easter Eggs

Ulysses Klaue's theft of vibranium from Wakanda is detailed early on in the film, explaining his possession of the metal in *Avengers: Age of Ultron* (2015). T'Chaka's death is reported in the news (a photo of Zemo is shown as part of the report) with scenes of T'Chaka and T'Challa from *Captain America: Civil War* used as flashbacks. Erik says he will arm Wakandan spies in Hong Kong, London, and New York; whether a coincidence or not, these are the three cities that contain Sanctum Sanctorums. When asked to heal Everett Ross, Shuri remarks that T'Challa has brought her another white boy to save, the first being Bucky, who we later see in the post-credits scene, cured of his Winter Soldier programming.

Chopped, Changed, and Lengthened

- According to Ryan Coogler, in early drafts of the screenplay Killmonger requests to be buried in Wakanda. It was Boseman who put forth the notion that Killmonger should ask to be buried elsewhere.
- A shot of Black Panther retrieving the EMP beads was filmed but cut out due to pacing reasons. (The beads were used earlier in the scene where he meets up with Nakia during her mission in Nigeria.)
- We see a young T'Challa and Nakia run through the tunnels in the City of the Dead. They spot T'Chaka, who beckons his son to come forth. T'Chaka tells T'Challa he had to make a difficult choice today, with the young boy replying that he's sure he did what was right for Wakanda. The scene then cuts to the present day, with the adult T'Challa looking upon the body of his deceased father.
- After T'Challa ingests the heart-shaped herb, he and Zuri reminisce about T'Chaka. T'Challa recalls seeing his father as the Black Panther, the time his father handed the mantle to him, as well as telling his father to not speak at the UN.
- T'Challa, Okoye, Shuri, and Nakia sneaks Everett Ross into T'Chaka's office. With the others having left the room, Nakia and Ross converse,

the pair talking about their personal lives. Ross surmises Nakia used to be in a relationship with T'Challa and reveals that he's divorced but isn't ready to take off his ring.
- Okoye and W'Kabi discuss T'Challa's loss to Killmonger, with W'Kabi expressing his anger that T'Challa didn't keep his promise to bring Klaue back to Wakanda. They then talk about what kind of world their children will grow up in.
- T'Challa, Nakia, Okoye, and Ayo walk through the lobby of the United Nations in Vienna, Austria. Everett Ross comes to greet them and proceeds to talk privately with T'Challa, trying to persuade him to not open Wakanda up to the world. T'Challa, though, remains adamant.

Location, Location

Wheat Street Towers serves as **N'Jobu's apartment**. It's located at 375 Auburn Avenue NE in Atlanta, Georgia, not Oakland, California, as the film implies. The **Museum of Great Britain** doesn't actually exist, with Atlanta's High Museum of Art (1280 Peachtree Street NE) filling in for the fictional locale. While **Warrior Falls** was built as a set at OFS'

Victoria Falls

global headquarters (2000 Northeast Expressway, Norcross, Georgia), Australia's Jim Jim Falls, South America's Iguazú Falls, and Africa's Oribi Gorge and Victoria Falls were used as reference and inspiration. The **throne room** was a set built at EUE/Screen Gems Studios Atlanta (175 Lakewood Way SW, Atlanta).

The story then moves over to South Korea, with the establishing shot featuring the city of Busan itself. It's back to Atlanta, though, with the subsequent **Jagalchi Fish Market street** filmed at the MET Atlanta, also known as the Metropolitan Business and Arts District (675 Metropolitan Parkway SW). After a tussle in the **illegal casino** (the set constructed on Stage 7 of EUE/Screen Gems Studios Atlanta), the Wakandans pursue Klaue and his men throughout the city, shot on location. **Nakia and Okoye follow Klaue** down Jagalchi-ro (passing the intersection with Jagalchi-ro 23beon-gil/Jagalchi-ro 24beon-gil). After passing underneath a parking complex, **Klaue and his men**

Gwangan Bridge

split off, with Nakia following the vehicles that went right, continuing on Jagalchi-ro. **Shuri directs the car she's controlling down a short cut**, which sees the vehicle turning from Jagalchi-ro 59beon-gil onto Jagalchi-ro 47beon-gil. The subsequent shot sees **the SUVs Shuri is chasing going down a hill**, turning from Wachi-ro onto Cheonghakseo-ro. The **SUVs then cause car crashes** to occur as they head west along Namhangsijang-gil, but **T'Challa manages to steer the car he's riding** left onto Yeongseon-daero. The action continues down Yeongseon-daero before they reach the entrance to Namhang Bridge. Cutting back to Nakia and Okoye, we see them chasing after the SUVs going west along Jagalchi-ro (when the scene starts, we see them go through the intersection at Jagalchi-ro 47beon-gil). **Okoye throws her spear causing one of the SUVs to crash** near the intersection at Jagalchi-ro 38beon-gil. Going back to T'Challa and Shuri, we find that they're on the 7.4-kilometre-long **Gwangan Bridge**. Crossing back to **Nakia and Okoye who are still in pursuit of Klaue**, we see them go over one hilly road and then another before Klaue destroys their car. The first was completed heading west on Jurye-ro near the KIT co-residence building, while the second hill section was filmed further down the same road in front of Dongseo University's Global Village building. We then cut back to T'Challa who's travelling north along Gwanganhaebyeon-ro, which runs parallel to Gwangalli Beach. We then see Klaue on Sajikbuk-ro 19beon-gil turning right onto Sajikbuk-ro, **destroying the car T'Challa was riding on** in the process. T'Challa runs across the side of a building and subsequently lands on Klaue's car, shredding one of its tires, causing it to flip (this last beat occurring on Sajikbuk-ro near the intersection with Sajikbuk-ro 5beon-gil). The area where **T'Challa finally confronts Klaue** was filmed on a backlot in Atlanta.

The **CIA South Korean black site** entrance can be found at 223 Mitchell St SW, Atlanta. The back of it, however, is a different building, with the filmmakers using the building that's directly across the road (206 Mitchell Street SW), with the alley Killmonger drives down being accessible from Nelson Street SW. After being rescued, Klaue is subsequently killed by Killmonger at an **airfield**, the filmmakers shooting at Atlanta Air Salvage (1146 Uniform Road, Griffin, Georgia).

The snowy mountain pass of **Jabari Land** was filmed at the Vulcan Materials Company quarry located at 3925 North Henry Boulevard, Stockbridge, Georgia. The **battle on Mount Bashenga** was filmed at Bouckaert Farm (9445 Browns Lake Road, Fairburn, Georgia) in Chattahoochee Hill country. Atlanta City Hall (55 Trinity Avenue SW, Atlanta) stands in for the **United Nations Office at Vienna**.

While none of *Black Panther* was actually shot in Africa, aerial footage of South Africa, Uganda (Rwenzori Mountains, Bwindi Impenetrable National Park), and Zambia was completed.

AVENGERS: INFINITY WAR

Directors: Anthony and Joe Russo
Screenplay: Christopher Markus & Stephen McFeely

Producer: Kevin Feige
Executive Producers: Louis D'Esposito, Victoria Alonso, Michael Grillo, Trinh Tran, Jon Favreau, James Gunn, and Stan Lee
Co-Producer: Mitch Bell
Associate Producers: JoAnn Perritano, Jen Underdahl, and Ari Costa

Cinematography: Trent Opaloch
Production Design: Charles Wood
Editing: Jeffrey Ford and Matthew Schmidt
Music: Alan Silvestri
Costume Design: Judianna Makovsky
Visual Effects Supervisor: Dan Deleeuw
Casting: Sarah Halley Finn

Production Company: Marvel Studios
Distribution Company: Walt Disney Studios Motion Pictures

US Release Date: 27 April 2018
Running Time: 149 minutes
Budget: $300–400 million
Box Office: $2,048,359,754

Based on the Marvel Comics by Stan Lee and Jack Kirby

Cast: Robert Downey Jr (*Tony Stark/Iron Man*), Chris Hemsworth (*Thor*), Mark Ruffalo (*Bruce Banner/Hulk*), Chris Evans (*Steve Rogers/Captain America*), Scarlett Johansson (*Natasha Romanoff/Black Widow*), Don Cheadle (*James Rhodes/War Machine*), Benedict Cumberbatch (*Doctor Strange*), Tom Holland (*Peter Parker/Spider-Man*), Chadwick Boseman (*T'Challa/Black Panther*), Zoe Saldana (*Gamora*), Karen Gillan (*Nebula*), Tom Hiddleston (*Loki*), Paul Bettany (*Vision*), Elizabeth Olsen (*Wanda Maximoff/Scarlet Witch*), Anthony Mackie (*Sam Wilson/Falcon*), Sebastian Stan (*Bucky Barnes/Winter Soldier*), Idris Elba (*Heimdall*), Danai Gurira (*Okoye*), Peter Dinklage (*Eitri*), Benedict Wong (*Wong*), Pom Klementieff (*Mantis*), Dave Bautista (*Drax*), Vin Diesel (*Groot*), Bradley Cooper (*Rocket*), Gwyneth Paltrow (*Pepper Potts*), Benicio del Toro (*The Collector*), Josh Brolin (*Thanos*), Chris Pratt (*Peter Quill/Star-Lord*), Sean Gunn (*On-Set Rocket*), William Hurt (*Secretary of State Thaddeus Ross*), Letitia Wright (*Shuri*), Terry Notary (*Cull Obsidian* and *On-Set Groot*), Tom Vaughan-Lawlor (*Ebony Maw*), Carrie Coon (*Proxima Midnight*), Michael Shaw (*Corvus Glaive*), Stan Lee (*Bus Driver*), Winston Duke (*M'Baku*), Florence Kasumba (*Ayo*), Kerry Condon (*FRIDAY*), Monique Ganderton (*On-Set Proxima Midnight*), Jacob Batalon (*Ned*), Tiffany Espensen (*Cindy*), Isabella Amara (*Sally*), Ethan Dizon (*Tiny*), Ariana Greenblatt (*Young Gamora*), Ameenah Kaplan (*Gamora's Mother*), Ross Marquand (*Red Skull (Stonekeeper)*), Stephen McFeely (*Secretary Ross' Aide*), Laura Miller (*Scottish News (STV) Reporter*), Samuel L Jackson (*Nick Fury*), Cobie Smulders (*Maria Hill*)

With Thanos unrelenting in his quest to gain the six Infinity Stones, the Avengers must come together and stop him from using the relics to wipe out half of all life in the universe.

It's all been leading to this. After eighteen films and the many appearances of the Infinity Stones, Marvel Studios were finally ready to adapt "The Infinity Gauntlet" story. Marvel Studios announced their Phase Three slate at an event at the El Capitan Theater in October 2014, setting a 4 May 2018 release for *Avengers: Infinity War – Part 1* and a 3 May 2019 release for *Avengers: Infinity War – Part II*.

In April 2015, Marvel officially announced Anthony and Joe Russo as the directors of the next two *Avengers* instalments. Joss Whedon, who helmed the first two *Avengers* films, declined to return to direct and write, given the difficulty he had behind the scenes when making *Avengers: Age of Ultron*

(2015) as well as citing the enormity of the project.

And so, in May 2015, Marvel announced that Christopher Markus and Stephen McFeely had been hired to write the screenplays to both parts of the film. The pair began by formulating ideas and brainstorming the different possibilities for both entries. Over the last four months of 2015, the writers worked out of a conference room, plotting out the first instalment on one wall, the second on another, with a third dedicated to cards of all the MCU characters (each card indicated whether or not the character could be used in the upcoming two *Avengers* films and had a rating on it—showing between one to five dollar signs—a rough indicator of that particular actor's fee which acted as a guide to how much it would cost to hire them). Other than mandating Thanos be featured, and in turn, the Infinity Stones, Marvel never stipulated that the writers had to kill off characters. Ideas for scenes and moments were written on cards and organised into a timeline from which Markus and McFeely compiled an outline. The writers began working on the actual scripts in January 2016. Drafts for both parts were completed by the time *Captain America: Civil War* was released on 6 May 2016. Owing to both movies telling different stories (as opposed to two halves of the one story), it was announced in July 2016 that *Part I* would simply be titled *Avengers: Infinity War*, with the new name for *Part II* to be revealed at a later time.

With development on the third and fourth *Avengers* films happening concurrently with the rollout of Phase Three, the directors and writers worked in conjunction with the filmmakers of other instalments to ensure a consistent continuity was kept between them. *Doctor Strange* director Scott Derrickson discussed the *Avengers* films with Joe and gave his feedback on the plot. James Gunn was consulted to ensure the Guardians of the Galaxy were authentic to how they're depicted in their two films. Scenes featuring Thor were rewritten to reflect the character's new comedic personality, with *Thor: Ragnarok* director Taika Waititi and Chris Hemsworth being flown in from Australia to discuss the new approach.

Given the sheer number of characters the films would have to focus on, many are split into smaller groups, with characters lumped together based on how interesting the resulting interactions would be. For example, the narcissistic personalities of Tony Stark—a man of science—and Stephen Strange—a sorcerer—were paired up to create conflict. Peter Quill and Spider-Man were added into the group for comic relief, with Spidey's presence also continuing the mentor/mentee relationship he has with Tony.

Thanos, meanwhile, would spend time with his daughter, Gamora, so their history could be explored. The Russo brothers likened *Infinity War* to a heist film, citing *2 Days in the Valley* (1996) and *Out of Sight* (1998) as inspiration.

As expected, much of the cast from the Marvel Cinematic Universe would return. Newcomers to the franchise include Peter Dinklage as Eitri, Hiroyuki Sanada as Akihiro, and Ross Marquand as the voice of the Red Skull. At D23 Expo 2017, it was revealed that the Children of Thanos would also make an appearance. The group consists of Carrie Coon as Proxima Midnight, Terry Notary as Cull Obsidian, Michael James Shaw as Corvus Glaive, and Tom Vaughan-Lawlor as Ebony Maw. To maintain secrecy, fake scenes were written and most of the cast members were not privy to the whole script.

Principal photography began on 23 January 2017 and wrapped on 14 July 2017. Although the initial plan was to shoot the two *Avengers* films simultaneously, it was decided instead to shoot them back-to-back to make it clear to the crew what scenes belonged to which film. Both *Infinity War* and its sequel were shot entirely using IMAX/Arri 2D digital cameras, making them the first Hollywood feature films to be shot entirely with IMAX cameras.

Since Thanos is an integral part of the story, it was paramount that the CGI character would appear believable, natural, and convey a wide range of emotions. To this end, the facial capture system Medusa was used to capture Josh Brolin doing a variety of expressions, which facilitated the creation of a digital Thanos. To portray Thanos on set, Brolin wore a motion capture suit as well as a facial capture head rig. To give his fellow actors the correct eye line, Brolin would either stand on a platform or wear a backpack with a pole extending from it. Thanos' design was changed from his previous appearances, incorporating more of Brolin's likeness and shifting the shade of his purple skin closer to pink. Weta Digital were tasked with Thanos' sequences on Titan whilst Digital Domain were responsible for animating the character on board the *Statesman*, his interactions with Gamora, and his appearance in Wakanda. Both companies initially produced their own model of Thanos, which culminated in visual effects supervisor Dan Deleeuw combining the elements he liked from both to form a consistent look for the character.

A large part of the third act takes place in Wakanda. Since *Black Panther* was not complete by the time production began on *Infinity War*, filmmakers on both projects were able to collaborate and ensure there was consistency in the way the African nation was depicted across the two films. Something that helped was both projects using the same location—Bouckaert Farm—for the large-scale Wakandan battle scenes. Arguably the biggest reveal in the film is that Thanos succeeds in not only assembling the Infinity Gauntlet but in his mission to wipe out half of all life in the universe. To preserve such a big twist, the cast were only told of their fates on the morning of the shoot. The original look of the characters disappearing involved digital light effects, tying into the fact that an Infinity Stone will light up when Thanos uses it. The visual effects team then trialled a light effect combined with a dusting effect, evolving into the final dusting effect seen in the film, which enabled the visual effects artists to preserve the actors' performances.

On 23 April 2018, *Avengers: Infinity War* had its world premiere at the Dolby Theatre in Hollywood. Marvel's years of careful planning paid off with the film setting a record for being the fastest to gross $1 billion, doing so in just eleven days—a record that would later be eclipsed by its sequel. Ending its run with a worldwide gross of over $2 billion, *Infinity War* ended up becoming the highest grossing film of 2018. Directors Anthony and Joe Russo and scribes Christopher Markus and Stephen McFeely manage to wrangle an incredibly complex concept and left viewers shocked, the film ending with the heroes defeated. Audiences had waited ten years for the Infinity Gauntlet to be assembled; they would need to wait a year longer to find out what the remaining Avengers would do.

Excelsior!

Stan Lee appears as a school bus driver, remarking that the kids on board are acting as if they've never seen a spaceship before.

Post-Credits Scene

Nick Fury and Maria Hill are driving down a road when a vehicle crashes in front of them. They quickly find that people around them are disappearing, including themselves. Before he fades away, Fury manages to activate a pager, with a white star on a blue and red background appearing on the screen.

Marvellous Miscellanea

- The filmmakers considered including characters from the Marvel-Netflix series in the film. Ultimately, it was decided not to feature any of them given how hard it was to correlate the stories of the shows and the movies.
- The film's working title during production was *Mary Lou 1* (with *Avengers: Endgame* going by *Mary Lou 2*). This is a reference to gymnast Mary Lou Retton who won a gold medal at the 1984 Olympics in Los Angeles,

becoming the first American woman to do so individually. In essence, Retton had stuck the landing, something the filmmakers of *Infinity War* and *Avengers: Endgame* had to do.

- *Thor* (2011) director Kenneth Branagh voiced the distress call heard during the film's opening, requesting nearby spaceships for aid as Thanos attacks the *Statesman*.
- Ebony Maw attempting to take the Eye of Agamotto from Doctor Strange and burning his hand is a nod to *Raiders of the Lost Ark* (1981), where the same thing happens to Arnold Ernst Toht as he picks up the headpiece to the Staff of Ra.
- The Guardians of the Galaxy have a new ship: the *Benatar*. It's named after singer Pat Benatar.
- Wanda Maximoff's Sokovian accent has noticeably faded and is sounding more American. The Russo brothers revealed this was an intentional choice, being the result of her spy training in *Captain America: Civil War* and the fact that she's been on the run prior to the events of *Infinity War*.
- An *Arrested Development* (2003-19) Easter egg can be spotted in the Collector's museum, with a blue-skinned Tobias Fünke on display in one of the cases. It's a reference to the episode "The One Where Michael Leaves" in which Fünke tries to join the Blue Man Group. The Russos tried to get David Cross to reprise his role but couldn't make it happen due to scheduling conflicts.
- Co-writer Stephen McFeely has a cameo in the film. He appears as part of the hologram meeting and can be seen on Secretary Ross' right.
- One of the funniest lines in the film, Drax's "I'll do you one better. Why is Gamora?" wasn't in the script. Chris Pratt suggested the line to Dave Bautista. Peter Quill's "For the record, this was my plan" which he says to the Avengers and other Guardians of the Galaxy who have Thanos restrained was another addition made by Pratt.
- Hugo Weaving was asked to return as the Red Skull but declined to do so. As such, Ross Marquand was hired instead. Marquand, known for his uncanny celebrity impressions, provided the character's voice, with the Red Skull being a CG creation this time around.
- During a test screening, an audience member referred to the Outriders as "space dogs." The filmmakers liked the term and wrote it in for Rocket to say during the battle in Wakanda.
- James Gunn has revealed that Groot's final line translates to "Dad."

- To prevent spoilers, a majority of the cast were not given the entire script to read, and fake scenes were written in case of leaks. These include the following: Loki creating an illusion of himself to distract Thanos while the real Loki sneaks away, saving only himself; Gamora surviving the throw off the cliff; and the Vision remaining operational after Thanos removes the Mind Stone from his head.
- After the release of *Infinity War*, the Russos revealed to HuffPost that, although we don't see them on-screen, Betty Ross, Sif, and the Asgardian actor who portrayed Loki all died when Thanos snapped his fingers.
- To celebrate the release of *Infinity War*, five of the six original Avengers actors got matching tattoos (Mark Ruffalo being the one who opted not to get inked). The design features a stylised 'A' superimposed with a '6'.

From Panels to the Screen

In the comics, Thanos is an Eternal, the son of A'Lars and Sui-San. The Eternals—a race created from the Celestials' experiments on humans—lived on Titan (a moon of Saturn in the source material; a planet in the film) and were wiped out when Thanos attacked his homeworld. In addition to being highly intelligent, Thanos is incredibly strong, has demonstrated some psychic abilities, and can fire blasts of energy.

While *Avengers: Infinity War* takes its name from "The Infinity War" story (*The Infinity War* #1-6, 1992), the film actually adapts two other storylines: "The Thanos Quest" (*The Thanos Quest* #1-2, 1990) and "The Infinity Gauntlet" (*The Infinity Gauntlet* #1-6, 1991). "The Thanos Quest" sees Thanos gathering the six Infinity Gems. He obtains the Soul Gem from the In-Betweener, the Power Gem from the Champion, the Time Gem from the Gardener, the Space Gem from the Runner, the Reality Gem from the Collector, and the Mind Gem from the Grandmaster. We then see many of Earth's heroes go up against the Titan in "The Infinity Gauntlet."

In the comics, Thanos gathers the Infinity Gems in an effort to woo Death, who has tasked him with eliminating half the population of the universe to balance out the fact that the number of beings currently alive outweighs all those that had ever died. The cinematic incarnation of Thanos forms the Infinity Gauntlet to aid him in his misguided mission to save the universe from overpopulation, a problem that previously led to the extinction of the Titan race.

The opening pages of *The Infinity Gauntlet* #1 sees Mephisto telling Thanos,

"My humble personage bows before your grandeur," a line echoed by Ebony Maw on-screen. The Hulk crashing through the Sanctum Sanctorum is also taken from this first chapter, although in the issue it's the Silver Surfer who warns Doctor Strange of the purple Titan's arrival. Though he doesn't do so in quite the same way as his screen counterpart, the comic book version of Thanos does torture Nebula throughout "The Infinity Gauntlet" story arc, beginning in this issue by resurrecting her with a disfigured body, keeping her partly dead and alive. Lastly, Thanos snapping his fingers to wipe out half the universe's population is also taken from *The Infinity Gauntlet* #1.

On Knowhere, Thanos turns Drax into cubes and Mantis into ribbons, with Starfox and Nebula having suffered those same fates respectively in *The Infinity Gauntlet* #2. Spider-Man firing a web into Thanos' face happens in *The Infinity Gauntlet* #4, as does the moment where Spider-Man is slammed into the ground (the issue sees Terraxia do this instead of the Titan). *Avengers: Infinity War* ends with Thanos smiling as he watches the sunset on an unidentified planet, recreating a similar scene from *The Infinity Gauntlet* #6.

Elements from "Infinity"—another story featuring Thanos—are also used (the core story occurs across *Infinity* #1-6, 2013). It is during "Infinity" that the Black Order makes their first full appearance. The Black Order—also known as the Cull Obsidian—is a group formed by Thanos to aid him in destroying worlds and forcing the inhabitants to pay tribute to the Titan. The group consists of Corvus Glaive (wields a blade that can cut atoms and prevents him from being killed as long as it remains intact), Proxima Midnight (a formidable warrior and Corvus Glaive's wife), Ebony Maw (a master manipulator with powers of persuasion; the film incarnation has telekinetic powers), Black Dwarf (super strong and has unbreakable skin; the MCU version is named Cull Obsidian), and Supergiant (possesses the ability to control minds; not present in the film). Also taken from the "Infinity" crossover storyline is the invasion of Wakanda (Thanos' armies head there to track down an Infinity Gem) and Ebony Maw manipulating Doctor Strange (doing so in order to find Thanos' son, Thane). Black Panther punching Cull Obsidian in the movie recreates a panel from *New Avengers* #9 (2013), an issue that ties into the "Infinity" story.

Tony Stark tells Pepper Potts that they should name their son after her uncle, Morgan. In the comics, Morgan Stark is actually Tony's cousin, who is envious of his fortune and has been a part of several plots to defeat him. In the film, Tony leans on the Cauldron of the Cosmos, a mystical artefact owned by Doctor Strange in the comics that allows him to peer through time. Ebony Maw arriving in New York to confront Doctor Strange is taken from *New Avengers* #8 (2013), one of several issues that serve as a prelude to "Infinity."

Iron Man's Mark 50 suit is based off two suits from the source material: the Bleeding Edge armour (a self-repairing suit composed of nano-machines contained within Tony's bones when not required) and the Model-Prime armour (composed of hexagonal scales that enabled it to shape-shift, creating things such as additional thrusters and weapons).

Likewise, Spider-Man's new suit in the film takes elements from two different costumes from the comics. The light-up lenses come from the Spider-Armor Mark 4 and the mechanical arms are taken from the Iron Spider suit (in the source material there are three arms and the costume has a red and gold colour scheme, whereas the MCU suit has four arms and is red, blue, and gold-coloured). And we finally see the MCU Peter Parker become an Avenger, with his comic book counterpart joining the team—specifically the New Avengers—in *The New Avengers* #3 (2005).

While Thor mistaking Rocket for a rabbit might just appear to be a joke, it may very well be a reference to the time Blackjack O'Hare (an anthropomorphic rabbit) impersonated Rocket Raccoon in the comics. Gamora's adoption is recounted by Thanos himself in *Warlock* #10 (1975). In the issue, it's revealed that the Church of Universal Truth wiped out the Zen-Whoberi, with Gamora being the sole survivor. Thanos then takes her in, raising her aboard his ship the *Sanctuary*.

While he doesn't quite use the name, Steve Rogers in the film essentially takes on his Nomad identity from the comics. Steve became disillusioned about his role after learning that the leader of the Secret Empire was a US government official. Giving up the Captain America mantle, he's later convinced to take on a new name and costume, becoming Nomad. Natasha Romanoff has blond hair in the film, a possible reference to another Black Widow in the comics, Yelena Belova.

Doctor Strange appears to use the Crimson Bands of Cyttorak to restrain Thanos. While they appear in the film as they do in the comic books, another artefact in the MCU—the restraints that trap Kaecilius in the New York Sanctum—is already known by this name. The spell Strange uses to duplicate himself is known in the source material as the Images of Ikonn.

In both media, Eitri is a blacksmith from Nidavellir. While both incarnations are Dwarves, in the comics he's quite short, with a height of four feet and seven inches (1.4 metres), whereas in the film he's depicted taller than Thor. Thor's new weapon, Stormbreaker, actually belongs to Beta Ray Bill in the comics. With Beta Ray Bill being worthy enough to lift Mjolnir, Eitri forged Stormbreaker for the Korbinite warrior at the behest of Odin. The hammer has similar properties to Mjolnir and is made from the same metal: uru. Stormbreaker's appearance in the MCU, however, seems to be based off the weapon Thor uses in the Ultimate Universe continuity.

Thanos locates the Soul Stone on Vormir. In the comics, the planet is home to the Vorms, a reptilian-like race. After he wipes out half of all sentient life in the universe, Thanos finds himself with a young Gamora in a pinkish orange-coloured landscape. This may be the MCU's version of Soul World, a pocket dimension that exists within the Soul Gem where the souls of those captured by the Gem reside.

Thanos' army largely comprises of Outriders, who are a genetically engineered race created to serve their master in the comics. Thanos taking the Mind Stone from Vision's forehead recalls the moment from *The Infinity Gauntlet* #4 when the Titan rips out Vision's internal circuitry. Additionally, when the Mind Stone is removed, the colour drains from Vision, a possible reference to the white look the android had for a time after being rebuilt in the source material, having been disassembled and his memory wiped by the organisation Vigilance.

In the comics, the Infinity Gems were destroyed in the lead up to the "Secret Wars" story (*Secret Wars* #1-9, 2015-16), an event that saw the destruction of the multiverse. In a case of the films influencing the source material, once the multiverse was restored, the Gems—now referred to as Infinity Stones—were brought back, their colours now matching their MCU counterparts (a yellow Mind Stone, a purple Power Stone, a red Reality Stone, an orange Soul Stone, a blue Space Stone, a green Time Stone).

MCU Easter Eggs

Loki tells Thanos that they "have a Hulk" and we get another appearance from the Chitauri and Leviathans, this time in flashback, which are both callbacks to *The Avengers* (2012). Bruce Banner uses the phone Steve Rogers gave Tony Stark from *Captain America: Civil War*, and the Sokovia Accords are referenced by Rhodey in his conversation with Thaddeus Ross. When Tony admits that he doesn't know where Vision is, Bruce exclaims, "Tony, you lost another super bot?" referring to Ultron and the plot of *Avengers: Age of Ultron*.

It's mentioned that Scott Lang and Clint Barton are absent as they are under house arrest. When Iron Man finds out that Spider-Man has gotten involved with the alien invasion, he tells him that this isn't like his adventure at Coney Island, a nod to the climactic battle of *Spider-Man: Homecoming*.

Drax mentions to Iron Man that Peter Quill once saved the universe with a dance off (as seen in 2014's *Guardians of the Galaxy*). The events from *Thor: Ragnarok*—namely the death of Odin and the revelation that he had a half-sister, Hela—are recounted by Thor to the Guardians of the Galaxy, with Quill responding he had to kill his father (as we saw in *Guardians of the Galaxy Vol. 2*). On their way to Nidavellir, Thor mentions to Rocket that his mother was killed by a Dark Elf, which happened in *Thor: The Dark World* (2013). We find out that the Red Skull was transported to Vormir after physically handling the Tesseract in *Captain America: The First Avenger* (2011). Okoye mentions how T'Challa has opened up Wakanda to the world, something that happened at the end of *Black Panther*. And finally, before he disappears, Nick Fury sends out a signal on a pager that displays the emblem of Captain Marvel.

Chopped, Changed, and Lengthened

- A backstory for Thanos was created during the script's development. Various stages of the character's life would have been shown, such as when he was a baby and a teenager, as well as his suggestion to the Titan government to kill half the population to solve their issue of overpopulation, for which he is sent to prison.
- A previous draft of the script was non-linear in structure, had Thanos narrating the film, and provided some background to the Black Order.
- Thanos attacking Xandar to retrieve the Power Stone was written but was cut from the script and wasn't filmed. It was felt the sequence served a similar purpose to the scene on Knowhere (Thanos and Gamora would have crossed paths) and they didn't want to repeat themselves.
- Had the sequence of Loki sneaking off the *Statesman* been used in *Thor: Ragnarok*, Thanos would have tracked Loki and the Tesseract to Jotunheim instead in *Infinity War*.
- An action scene set during Steve Rogers', Natasha Romanoff's, and Sam Wilson's time on the run was written. There was also a moment where, having finished fighting some criminals, Steve is eating mashed potatoes. Sam then points out that Steve is bleeding into his food. According

to Christopher Markus, Kevin Feige did not approve of this particular scene.
- An early version of the screenplay included a sequence where the Black Order attacked the New York Sanctum. During the battle, Black Widow, Bruce Banner, and Wong find themselves in the Mindscape where they're made to experience their worst fears.
- During Doctor Strange's fight with Thanos on Titan, the sorcerer sends his opponent on a mind trip, with Thanos encountering his various victims (one sequence sees them grabbing onto him) before appearing in front of the Living Tribunal (the judge of the multiverse in the comics) who deems him to be guilty. Thanos, however, figures out it's all a ruse. It was reasoned that introducing the idea of an all-powerful being that didn't deal with Thanos made little sense, and since it also ruined the pace of the battle, the scene was cut. It's unconfirmed if the scene was shot.
- Originally, Thor, Rocket, and Groot would have journeyed to the location where Thor's ancestors had slain the World Serpent, with Stormbreaker still buried in the dead serpent's skull. They would have then fought off the World Serpent's children in order to escape. This idea was scrapped as it didn't advance the characters' stories and so the sequence with Eitri was conceived in its place.
- An appearance by Howard the Duck was written in at one point. He would have been playing poker when Peter Quill finds him to get some information. The scene would also have included a cameo appearance by Ken Jeong.
- A draft of the script saw Steve Rogers introduced much later into the film, tackling Corvus Glaive off Vision during the battle in Wakanda. It was felt that the moment wasn't really satisfying, and so Steve's introduction was rewritten to occur much earlier in *Infinity War*.
- Other concepts explored in drafts include Tony Stark and Steve Rogers reuniting and dealing with their fallout from *Captain America: Civil War*, Falcon heading into space instead of Spider-Man, and Nick Fury being snapped away at a train station.
- The scene with Tony and Pepper talking in Central Park was originally longer, with Happy Hogan driving by in a buggy complaining to the couple that they should just elope as he's having a hard time keeping the media away. Happy then spots a photographer (played by Joe Russo) nearby and proceeds to chase him away. The sequence was cut to increase the pace of the scene.

- An alternate scene introducing Tony and Pepper was shot during additional photography. It would have seen Tony at home playing with the flip phone Steve gave him, with Pepper subsequently entering the room and Doctor Strange making an appearance. The filmmakers preferred the park scene as they felt it had more energy and so they kept it.
- During the battle in Scotland, Wanda Maximoff and Vision attempt to hide from Corvus Glaive and Proxima Midnight but are eventually found by the pair.
- At one point during the Q Ship sequence, Tony would have transferred the Iron Man armour over to Doctor Strange to protect him from Ebony Maw's needles, with Tony subsequently donning the Cloak of Levitation.
- Still on Knowhere after their encounter with Thanos, we find Peter Quill listening to "New York Groove" by Ace Frehley on board the *Benatar* until Drax turns off the Zune. The pair argue until Mantis interrupts them, pointing out that the coded message channel light is blinking. Quill begins to chastise Mantis for not pointing it out earlier but quickly realizes it was Drax's job to do so. Drax replies saying that he did see the yellow light but that Quill told him "if it was yellow, let it mellow; brown, flush it down." Quill checks the messages and finds that Nebula has sent them coordinates to Titan.
- Onboard the *Sanctuary II*, Thanos recreates a moment from his past (Gamora informing him that a planet has been taken and will now be loyal to Thanos) using the Reality Stone for Gamora to see. She tells him to stop the illusion. Thanos says he raised her to be a warrior. Gamora retorts that she didn't ask to be raised that way. Thanos reveals that he knows she found the location of the Soul Stone and that she lied about doing so, going on to assert that she didn't escape from him; rather, he let her leave.
- On Titan, Doctor Strange tasks Spider-Man with rescuing the Guardians of the Galaxy whose bodies have been scattered all over the place after Thanos separated their souls from their bodies. Spidey brings them over to Mantis—who he has already rescued—and tells her to revive them.
- Bruce Banner, who's suited up in the Hulkbuster, is fighting Cull Obsidian. He makes a deal with the Hulk to merge their personalities together. This new "Smart Hulk" then bursts out of the Hulkbuster. He attaches a boot from the armour to Cull Obsidian, sending him flying up towards the force field and dying. The scene ultimately wasn't used as its victorious nature was at odds with the losses the heroes would come to suffer.

- In Wakanda, Smart Hulk comes across Natasha and Falcon. Natasha starts her lullaby but Bruce speaks, explaining to a shocked Natasha he has merged his personality with the Hulk's.
- Several shots used in the *Infinity War* trailers aren't present in the final film: Tony saying "Wow" after Quill proposes to come up with a plan to defeat Thanos; Bruce standing next to a Hulkbuster arm in Wakanda; Bruce, Black Widow, and War Machine standing together looking up; Steve activating one of the shields T'Challa has given him (before he heads out to the battlefield); and Thor summoning lightning at Nidavellir with Rocket and Groot observing him. A key shot from the trailer created specifically for marketing and never intended to be used in the movie sees War Machine, Bucky, Black Widow, Steve Rogers, the Hulk, Okoye, Falcon, and Black Panther running towards the camera in Wakanda. We also don't hear Thanos utter the line "Fun isn't something one considers when balancing the universe, but this does put a smile on my face," which was replaced by a different one in post-production. To preserve the fact that Thanos had acquired most of the Infinity Stones by that point, in the shot of Steve pushing back against Thanos' left hand the Infinity Gauntlet is depicted with only the Space and Power Stones. In a promotional featurette for the film, Star-Lord holds up a fist to Thanos, instead of giving him the finger.

Location, Location

Filming on *Infinity War* primarily took place in the US state of Georgia. After Bruce Banner crashes back to Earth, we cut to Tony Stark and Pepper Potts walking in **Central Park**. Atlanta's Piedmont Park stands in for the iconic New York landmark, with shooting taking place near the Peace Monument (the sports fields in the distance were digitally replaced with water). When Doctor Strange appears via a portal, it's the gates to the 14th Street entrance (off Piedmont Avenue) that we see behind him. Iron Man, Doctor Strange, and Wong initially face off against Ebony Maw and Cull Obsidian on a **New York Street**. Atlanta's Walton Street (between Cone Street NW and Forsyth Street NW) was dressed to look like a street in the Big Apple. Woodruff Park stands in for **Washington Square Park**, where Iron Man, with a little help from Spider-Man, fights Cull Obsidian.

Catching up with Wanda Maximoff and Vision, we find the pair hanging out in Scotland, with filming completed on location. Going out for a walk,

Wanda and Vision see the news of New York being attacked on a television in **Hüsnü Kebab Grill House**. The restaurant is fictional, with the real location—Miss Katie Cupcake (52 Cockburn Street, Edinburgh)—actually selling jewellery and gifts. Corvus Glaive and Proxima Midnight then attack the pair, with Wanda being thrown through the window of **Laila's Mediterranean Bistro** (63 Cockburn Street, Edinburgh). Wanda transports the injured Vision over to the **Edinburgh City Chambers** (253 High Street, Edinburgh). Catching up to them, Corvus Glaive takes Vision up to the roof of **St Giles' Cathedral** (High Street, Edinburgh), with Wanda fighting Proxima Midnight below in **Parliament Square**. The action moves to **Waverley Station** (near Platform 2), where we reunite with Steve Rogers, Black Widow, and Falcon.

St Giles' Cathedral

Brazil's Lençois Maranhenses National Park doubles as the landscape of **Vormir**, the location having been chosen due to its expansive sand dunes. The **battle in Wakanda** was filmed at Bouckaert Farm (9445 Browns Lake Road, Fairburn, Georgia) in Chattahoochee Hill country. The filmmakers brought in native African trees and created a river for filming. During the battle, Bruce Banner faces off against Cull Obsidian near a **waterfall**, with Hurricane Falls in Georgia's Tallulah Gorge State Park being used. Having accomplished his goal, Thanos retreats to his **farm**, with the filmmakers using plates of the Banaue Rice Terraces of the Philippines. The post-credits scene of **Maria Hill and Nick Fury disappearing** was filmed on Forsyth Street NW (between Luckie Street NW and Williams Street NW) in Atlanta. Sets were built at Pinewood Atlanta Studios (now known as Trilith Studios; 461 Sandy Creek Road, Fayetteville, Georgia), such as the ones for the *Statesman* and **Titan**.

ANT-MAN AND THE WASP

Director: Peyton Reed
Screenplay: Chris McKenna & Erik Sommers and Paul Rudd & Andrew Barrer & Gabriel Ferrari

Producers: Kevin Feige and Stephen Broussard
Executive Producers: Louis D'Esposito, Victoria Alonso, Charles Newirth, and Stan Lee
Co-Producers: Mitch Bell and Lars P Winther
Associate Producers: Laura Stoltz and Kevin R Wright

Cinematography: Dante Spinotti
Production Design: Shepherd Frankel
Editing: Dan Lebental and Craig Wood
Music: Christophe Beck
Costume Design: Louise Frogley
Visual Effects Supervisor: Stephane Ceretti
Casting: Sarah Halley Finn

Production Company: Marvel Studios
Distribution Company: Walt Disney Studios Motion Pictures

US Release Date: 6 July 2018
Running Time: 118 minutes
Budget: $162–195 million
Box Office: $622,674,139

Based on the Marvel Comics by Stan Lee, Larry Lieber, and Jack Kirby

Cast: Paul Rudd (*Scott Lang/Ant-Man*), Evangeline Lilly (*Hope van Dyne/Wasp*), Michael Peña (*Luis*), Walton Goggins (*Sonny Burch*), Bobby Cannavale (*Paxton*), Judy Greer (*Maggie*), Tip "TI" Harris (*Dave*), David Dastmalchian (*Kurt*), Hannah John-Kamen (*Ava Starr/Ghost*), Abby Ryder Fortson (*Cassie*), Randall Park (*Jimmy Woo*), Michelle Pfeiffer (*Janet van Dyne/Wasp*), Laurence Fishburne (*Dr Bill Foster*), Michael Douglas (*Dr Hank Pym*), Divian Ladwa (*Uzman*), Goran Kostic (*Anitolov*), Rob Archer (*Knox*), Sean Thompson Kleier (*Agent Stoltz*), Benjamin Byron Davis (*Agent Burleigh*), Michael Cerveris (*Elihas Starr*), Riann Steele (*Catherine Starr*), Dax Griffin (*Young Hank*), Hayley Lovitt (*Young Janet*), Langston Fishburne (*Young Bill*), Raelynn Bratten (*Young Ava*), Madeleine McGraw (*Young Hope*), Tim Heidecker (*Whale Boat Captain Daniel Gooobler*), Stan Lee (*Shrinking Car Owner*), Suehyla El-Attar (*Agent Pearson*), Julia Vera Andrews (*Luis' Abuelita*)

With his house arrest almost at an end, Scott Lang finds himself drawn back into the role of Ant-Man when Hank Pym and Hope van Dyne ask for his assistance in rescuing Janet van Dyne from the Quantum Realm.

In October 2015, Marvel Studios announced that *Ant-Man* (2015) would receive a sequel—*Ant-Man and the Wasp*—with a release date of 6 July 2018. This marks the first Marvel Cinematic Universe film with a female hero in the title. Peyton Reed returned to direct, along with stars Paul Rudd, Evangeline Lilly, and Michael Douglas.

With *Avengers: Infinity War* ending on a bleak note, it was appropriate then for Marvel Studios' next film to be a palate cleanser—one with humour, action, and a bit of romance. Continuing a storyline from the first film, *Ant-Man and the Wasp* sees Scott Lang, Hope van Dyne, and Hank Pym searching for Janet van Dyne. With the characters on a time-sensitive mission, Reed looked to the comedy films *After Hours* (1985) and *Midnight Run* (1988) as inspiration on the movie's tone. The director also made it a goal to feature more of San Francisco, a location that had yet to be fully explored in the MCU.

Michelle Pfeiffer was cast as Janet, being Reed's go-to choice for the role. In fact, when the filmmakers were casting the role of Janet for *Ant-Man*, Hayley Lovitt was chosen due to her large eyes that bore a resemblance to Pfeiffer's. Pfeiffer had previously portrayed the comic book character Selina Kyle/Catwoman in *Batman Returns* (1992).

Laurence Fishburne landed the role of Bill Foster, a former colleague of

Hank Pym's. A fan of comic books, this wouldn't be Fishburne's first comic book movie role, having previously voiced the Silver Surfer in *Fantastic Four: Rise of the Silver Surfer* (2007) and portraying Perry White in both *Man of Steel* (2013) and *Batman v Superman: Dawn of Justice* (2016). *Fresh Off the Boat* (2015-20) actor Randall Park joined the cast as FBI agent Jimmy Woo.

Antagonists for the film came in the form of Walton Goggins' Sonny Birch—a gangster dealing in black market tech—and Hannah John-Kamen's Ava Starr/Ghost—a former stealth operative with the ability to phase through objects. In the comics, little is known about Ghost (who's male in the source material), giving the filmmakers free reign to craft a character to fit within the film's story. Principal photography began on 1 August 2017, with production once again based at Pinewood Atlanta Studios, and was completed on 19 November 2017.

A central location to the film's story was Hank Pym's portable laboratory. The multi-storey set took seventeen weeks to complete and was surrounded by a green screen curtain. Various over-sized objects were created—clothes pegs, Lego pieces, radio dials—to decorate the lab, reflecting Hank's ingenuity. This was also to disorient audiences, making them question whether or not the characters have shrunk or if small objects have been enlarged. The quantum tunnel was created with LED lights built in and its design was based off the time machine from *The Time Tunnel* (1966-67).

Hope is finally given the chance to suit up and prove herself, with audiences seeing Wasp in action for the first time in a thrilling sequence set in a restaurant. Evangeline Lilly wanted Wasp's fighting style to be fluid and graceful. She trained in boxing and kickboxing and worked with stunt doubles Ingrid Kleinig and Renae Moneymaker on the choreography. Owing to their large depth of field, the macro photography unit utilized Frazier lenses to depict the world when Wasp is in miniature form. Various methods were often used to create a single shot. When one of Sonny's men throws a knife at Hope, a high frame rate was used to capture the actor miming the action of the throw (the knife later added in digitally) allowing the filmmakers to slow down the footage and increase the drama of the moment. Wasp's subsequent jump and shrink was a combination of motion-captured footage and CGI.

Ant-Man and the Wasp had its world premiere at the El Capitan Theatre in Los Angeles on 25 June 2018. Director Peyton Reed finally got a chance to really show off the franchise's potential, building on the humour and light-hearted fun from the first instalment. Critics praised the action and visual effects, with many appreciating the tender moments between characters. While not the biggest hit at the box office, *Ant-Man and the Wasp* was a great shift in tone from the grand scale of *Avengers: Infinity War*.

Excelsior!
During the chase through San Francisco, Hope accidentally shrinks Stan Lee's car. He remarks that "Well, the '60s were fun, but now I'm paying for it." Many different versions of Lee reacting to his car shrinking were filmed. These include: "Talk about compact cars!", "Well, at least now I'll be able to park in San Francisco," "Oh, man. I just stole this car," "Well, looks like I'm walking," and "Everything is shrinking on me."

Mid-Credits Scene
Scott heads into the Quantum Realm to retrieve some quantum healing particles. Finished with his task, he's about to be pulled out, but finds he's still in the Quantum Realm, with Hank, Janet, and Hope having disappeared due to Thanos using the Infinity Gauntlet.

Post-Credits Scene
The enlarged ant that is in Scott's home can be seen playing an electronic drum kit.

Marvellous Miscellanea
- The working title for the film was *Cherry Blue*. The name is a reference to a sketch from *Check It Out! with Dr. Steve Brule* (2010-17) in which the titular character wants to buy a cherry-red-coloured car but could only afford a cherry-blue-coloured one.
- The film's title refers to Scott Lang and Hope van Dyne as well as Hank Pym and Janet van Dyne.
- The movie Scott watches after he calls Hank is *National Lampoon's Animal House* (1978). The clip in question sees Larry Kroger discussing with Professor Dave Jennings how "our whole solar system could be, like, one tiny atom in the fingernail of some other giant being" and in turn how an atom in his own fingernail could be "one little tiny universe."
- One of the more obvious cinematic references in *Ant-Man and the Wasp* is its nod to *The Big Lebowski* (1998). In both films, the protagonist gets caught up in an adventure while clad in a bathrobe.

- Visual effects supervisor Stephane Ceretti has a cameo in the film. He can be seen opening the door to a restaurant after a garbage truck drives over the shrunken car Hope and Scott are in.
- To portray Ghost's unstable molecular body, multiple takes of Hannah John-Kamen's performance were composited together. Visual effects artists also created a digital double, with the translucent copy animated to display a different action or reaction, as if we're seeing alternate versions of the character.
- The classroom Scott enters to retrieve the old Ant-Man suit belongs to Mrs Broadwell. Mrs Broadwell was Peyton Reed's eighth and ninth grade English teacher.
- Langston Fishburne, Laurence Fishburne's son, doubled for his father in the flashback scenes, informing the visual effects team how to de-age Laurence for the final shot. Laurence's appearance in *Boyz n the Hood* (1991) and *Deep Cover* (1992) were also used as reference.
- The films *Bullitt* (1968) and *What's Up, Doc?* (1972) were used as inspiration for the car chase through the streets of San Francisco.
- After the post-credits scene, a message appears on screen stating, "Ant-Man and The Wasp will return." Moments after, however, a curved stroke appears above the full stop, transforming it into a question mark.
- In the UK, *Ant-Man and the Wasp* came out on 2 August 2018, a month after its release in the US. This was most likely done to avoid clashing with the 2018 FIFA World Cup. The fact that the Pixar film *Incredibles* 2 was also given a delayed UK release (the film came out on 15 June in the US, with the UK getting it on 13 July) was potentially another factor in the decision. The three-week gap between *Incredibles* 2 and *Ant-Man and the Wasp* ensured Disney would not compete against itself.

From Panels to the Screen
In the film, Scott Lang forms X-Con Security Consultants with Luis, Dave, and Kurt. The comic book incarnation of Scott also started his own company—Ant-Man Security Solutions.

Wasp's wings in the movie are not a part of her body as per the comics, but rather a part of the suit she wears. Additionally, Janet van Dyne being trapped in the Quantum Realm and subsequently rescued is an ordeal her comic book counterpart also experiences. In *Secret Invasion* #7 (2008), Janet—having consumed a serum given to her by the Skrull Criti Noll disguised as

Hank Pym—finds she has been turned into a weapon, her body growing and emanating noxious energy. To save everyone, Thor uses Mjolnir to transform Janet into energy (occurring in *Secret Invasion* #8, 2008). She is believed dead until, in *The Avengers* #32 (2012), it's revealed that she survived (Janet having shrunk herself down in her final moments), sending a signal to her fellow Avengers who travel to the Microverse to retrieve her.

In the film, Jimmy Woo is an FBI agent, a role his comic book counterpart also had before going on to work for S.H.I.E.L.D. The character's existence in the Marvel Cinematic Universe was previously hinted in the *Agents of S.H.I.E.L.D.* (2013-20) episode "Face My Enemy," where the name "Woo" appears in Melinda May's recent call list on her phone. The comic book version of Sonny Burch worked for Cross Technological Enterprises and became the US government's Under-Secretary for Acquisition, Technology, and Logistics. His cinematic incarnation has been reimagined as a restaurateur and someone who deals in black market tech.

In the comics, the Ghost is male (his true identity is a mystery), whereas the cinematic version is female (given the name Ava Starr). Otherwise, both incarnations have a similar skill set, being able to phase through solid matter and turn invisible. In the source material, however, the Ghost's abilities are derived from the suit itself. Both the MCU and comic book incarnations of Elihas Starr are scientists, but only in the film is he the Ghost's father. The comic book version is also known as Egghead due to his, well, egg-shaped head.

Both the screen and comic book incarnations of Bill Foster have worked with Hank Pym conducting research on Pym Particles. Bill reveals that he was partnered with Hank on a project called Goliath, a nod to one of the many names Bill has taken on in the source material. He started off with Black Goliath, took on the moniker of Giant-Man, before settling on Goliath. The character wears several items of blue clothing in the film, possibly a subtle nod to the presence of the colour in the character's costume in the comics. Project Goliath was previously referenced in an extended scene from *Iron Man 2* (2010): after Tony Stark rediscovers a new element, he tells JARVIS to get him "everything from Projects Pegasus, Exodus, and Goliath."

Cassie says to her father that she wishes she could fight bad guys. The comic book version of the character has done exactly that: taking on the name Stature, she possesses growing and shrinking powers and is a member of the Young Avengers. Kurt mentions Baba Yaga in the film. While he is most likely referring to the figure from Slavic folklore, it's worth noting that Baba Yaga does exist in the Marvel Universe, making her first appearance in *Captain Britain* #11 (1985).

As Hank and Janet leave the Quantum Realm, what appears to be a city in a dome can be spotted. In the comics, several worlds exist within the Microverse (the comic book equivalent of the Quantum Realm) such as K'ai, Kaliklak, and Spartak.

MCU Easter Eggs

The Avengers' clash at Leipzig/Halle Airport in Germany and the Sokovia Accords are mentioned by Jimmy Woo when he tries to explain to Cassie why Scott is under house arrest (in fact, the airport fight is brought up several times by different characters in the film). In the mid-credits scene, we see Hank, Janet, and Hope all turn to ash as a result of Thanos' finger snap in *Avengers: Infinity War*.

Chopped, Changed, and Lengthened

- Luis retelling the airport fight from *Captain America: Civil War* was an idea that was scrapped, with the filmmakers not wanting to reference the film too many times.
- It's 1987 and Hank Pym and Janet van Dyne are in Buenos Aires. They follow Elihas Starr through the city but lose him as he reaches his lab. The pair then suit up as Ant-Man and the Wasp and fight their way into the complex. Janet destroys the computers while Hank deals with Elihas directly and tries to stop him from using his quantum tunnel. Guards shoot at Hank, but he shrinks, with the bullets causing the tunnel to malfunction. Hank and Janet manage to escape before it explodes. The sequence was removed, as Reed wanted the focus to be on the main story set in the present.
- Sonny and his men are at a bookstore. The owner shows them footage from his security camera, which depicts Hank's lab shrinking. Other cameras in the area were covered with ants, but the bookstore owner had an exterminator spray his shop recently. Sonny orders his men to track down the lab before asking the storeowner if he has a first edition copy of *Dianetics*.
- Hank is in the Quantum Realm trying to find Janet. As he finds her, a creature with tentacles attacks him. Janet fights it, fending it off before reuniting properly with her husband.
- Hank and Janet encounter a large, semi-translucent creature in the Quan-

tum Realm. Janet uses a device that translates her words to communicate with the creature, letting it know that they just want to pass. The creature moves and allows them to continue on their way.

Location, Location

Once again, the house at 601 Buena Vista Avenue W, San Francisco, California, is used as **Hank Pym's home**. **Scott Lang's home** can be found at 1400 18th Street, San Francisco. The entrance we see in the film is located on Missouri Street.

Pigeons attack Hope's shrunken car on Broad Street NW in Atlanta, Georgia, close to the intersection with Walton Street NW (you can see the Best Cajun Asian restaurant in the background). The **vacant lot** where we first see Hank shrink his lab is a Douglas Parking space, specifically Lot 69 on Harrison Street (near 15th Street) in Oakland, California. With Hope going to meet with Sonny Burch, Hank and Scott wait in the van inside a **delivery dock**. The filmmakers used the Fairlie Street NW dock to the Central Library branch (1 Margaret Mitchell Square) of the Atlanta-Fulton Public Library System. Located in Downtown Atlanta, the building was designed by Marcel Breuer. Southern Exchange Ballrooms (200 Peachtree Street, Atlanta) stands in for the restaurant **Oui**.

The offices of **X-Con Security Consultants** can be found on the upper floor of 76 Peachtree Street, Atlanta. The **University of California, Berkeley** initially features as itself, with Hank, Hope, and Scott walking down Sather Road, with the Sather Gate in the background. Subsequent footage, however, was captured at Emory University (201 Dowman Drive, Atlanta). Goodrich C White Hall (301 Dowman Drive, Atlanta) was used for the Department of Physics, Math, and Astronomy, with Bill Foster's lecture being filmed in Room 208, while his office was erected in the lobby with temporary walls used.

Samuel M Inman Middle School (774 Virginia Avenue NE, Atlanta) stands in for the exterior of **Brookemont Elementary School**, with the interiors being shot at Atlanta International School (2890 North Fulton Drive, Atlanta). The house at 22 Woodlane Drive, Newnan, Georgia, was used as the exterior to **Ava Starr's residence**, with interiors being constructed as a set at Pinewood Atlanta Studios (now called Trilith Studios; 461 Sandy Creek Road, Fayetteville, Georgia). El Bandido Mex Mex Grill (1083 Euclid Avenue, Atlanta) was used as the **Mexican restaurant** Luis' *abuelita* owns. When Hope says, "I can't believe you split like that! Smell you later, dummy," during Luis' story, Hope is on **18th Street** between Connecticut Street and Missouri Street in San Francisco.

While it may look like **Muir Woods**, shooting actually occurred in a wooded area near Pinewood Atlanta Studios, with sequoias digitally added in. The building at 270 Peachtree Street NW in Atlanta is used as the **FBI office**, with Hank walking out of the fire exit on Baker Street NW. On their way to retrieve Hank's lab, Scott, Hope, and Hank head east along San Francisco's **Filbert Street** (between Jones Street and Taylor Street), following an arrow created by flying ants. The **empty lot** where our heroes ambush Ghost and Bill Foster was filmed in the Gulch area located in Downtown Atlanta (specifically in the area behind the Norfolk Southern Building at 125 Spring Street SW), an area previously used in *Captain America: Civil War*.

With Hope in possession of the lab, Sonny and his men give chase through the streets of San Francisco. We see them follow her down a hill on **Montgomery Street** (between Green Street and Vallejo Street). It's on the same street—this time between Broadway and Pacific Avenue—that Hope shrinks her vehicle, causing one of the pursuers to crash, before turning right onto Pacific Avenue. This takes place not too far from the Transamerica Pyramid (600 Montgomery Street), which can be seen in the scene. We then see the vehicles heading west on **California Street**, going through the intersection with Taylor Street. Hope shrinks down, goes underneath the pursuing vehicle, and enlarges again causing it to flip near the California Street and Jones Street intersection. Hope then leads the cars down the famous steep section of **Lombard Street** (between Hyde Street and Leavenwirth Street) with its hairpin turns. Portions of the action sequence were also filmed in Atlanta, which stood in for San Francisco. It's outside My Fair Sweets where **Stan Lee's car is shrunk** accidentally (231 Mitchell Street SW, Atlanta). **Ghost then enters the fray**, phasing through a car before knocking one of Sonny's men off his motorbike on Trinity Avenue SW (between Peachtree Street SW and Pryor Street SW). **Hope enlarges Luis' Hello Kitty Pez dispenser** at the Martin Luther King Jr Drive SW and Central Avenue SW intersection. **Ghost**

San Francisco, California

catches up to the van, phases through the windshield and knocks Hope out of the vehicle, the sequence being filmed on Mitchell Street SW (between Pryor Street SW and Central Avenue SW). **Scott abandons the crashed van** on Wall Street SW (between Pryor Street and Central Ave SW). **Hope, and soon after, Scott, catch up to Ghost** on Peachtree Street (between Martin Luther King Jr Drive SW and Alabama Street SW). **Hope is knocked off the truck**, with Ghost following her on Pryor Street SW (between Martin Luther King Jr Drive SW and Lower Alabama Street). **Scott brings the truck to a halt** on Peachtree Street (between Andrew Young International Boulevard NW and Ellis Street NE), passing a **café** (in actuality, Braves All-Star Grill at 200 Peachtree Street, Atlanta) with the customers inside oblivious to the events outside. We then see the actual San Francisco again, with Scott using the truck to skate down **Mason Street**, going through the Bush Street intersection. Now behind the wheel of a purple car selected from the Hot Wheels Rally case, Luis heads north on **Jones Street**, going through the intersection with Broadway. He drives his shrunken car over a hill, with a pursuing vehicle following him, which was filmed on Jones Street between Union Street and Green Street. The resulting pile-up occurs at the Jones Street and Filbert Street intersection. The shoot location zips back to Atlanta where **Scott catches up to Sonny**. The sequence was filmed on Forsyth Street SW, going through the intersection with Marietta St NW, with Scott kicking Sonny's vehicle before the Walton Street NW intersection. **Sonny then evades the enlarged Scott** by slipping into a narrow alleyway on Forsyth Street between 55 Marietta Street NW and the Forsyth-Walton Building (52 Walton Street). The part when Sonny emerges on the other end, however, was filmed back in San Francisco, with the alley next to Jack in the Box (2739 Taylor Street) being used.

Scott ends up in the **Fisherman's Wharf** area of San Francisco, specifically near Piers 41 and 43, before hitching a ride on an ant and continuing to catch up to Sonny. With a sighting of Scott having been reported, Agent Woo heads west on **Jackson Street** and turns right onto **Laguna Street**. He heads to the Broadway and Laguna Street intersection where he sees the **enlarged Ant-Man suit propped up** against 1999 Broadway. Ghost and Bill Foster hide from the authorities in **St Louis Alley**, located in San Francisco's Chinatown. **Maggie's house** is located at 840 Clemont Drive NE, Atlanta. Hank and Janet set up their home on **Kahana Bay Beach Park**, located on the island of Oahu, Hawaii.

The mid-credits scene with our heroes on the roof of a **parking complex** was filmed in Los Angeles, California, with the San Francisco skyline added in digitally behind them.

CAPTAIN MARVEL

Directors: Anna Boden and Ryan Fleck
Screenplay: Anna Boden & Ryan Fleck & Geneva Robertson-Dworet
Story: Nicole Perlman & Meg LeFauve and
Anna Boden & Ryan Fleck & Geneva Robertson-Dworet

Producer: Kevin Feige
Executive Producers: Louis D'Esposito, Victoria Alonso,
Jonathan Schwartz, Patricia Whitcher, and Stan Lee
Co-Producers: David J Grant and Lars P Winther

Cinematography: Ben Davis
Production Design: Andy Nicholson
Editing: Elliot Graham and Debbie Berman
Music: Pinar Toprak
Costume Design: Sanja Hays
Visual Effects Supervisor: Christopher Townsend
Casting: Sarah Halley Finn

Production Company: Marvel Studios
Distribution Company: Walt Disney Studios Motion Pictures

US Release Date: 8 March 2019
Running Time: 124 minutes
Budget: $152–175 million
Box Office: $1,128,462,972

Based on the Marvel Comics

Cast: Brie Larson (*Carol Danvers/Vers/Captain Marvel*), Samuel L Jackson (*Nick Fury*), Ben Mendelsohn (*Talos* and *Keller*), Jude Law (*Yon-Rogg*), Annette Bening (*Supreme Intelligence* and *Dr Wendy Lawson*), Djimon Hounsou (*Korath*), Lee Pace (*Ronan*), Lashana Lynch (*Maria Rambeau*), Gemma Chan (*Minn-Erva*), Clark Gregg (*Agent Coulson*), Rune Temte (*Bron-Char*), Algenis Perez Soto (*Att-Lass*), Mckenna Grace (*Young Carol (13 Years Old)*), Akira Akbar (*Monica Rambeau (11 Years Old)*), Matthew Maher (*Norex*), Chuku Modu (*Soh-Larr*), Colin Ford (*Steve Danvers*), Kenneth Mitchell (*Joseph Danvers*), Pete Ploszek (*Bret Johnson*), Matthew "Spider" Kimmel (*Spider*), Stephen "Cajun" Del Bagno (*Cajun*), London Fuller (*Young Carol (6 Years Old)*), Azari Akbar (*Monica Rambeau (5 Years Old)*), Barry Curtis (*Mall Security Guard*), Marilyn Brett (*Older Lady on Train*), Stan Lee (*Stan Lee*), Robert Kazinsky (*Biker (The Don)*), Sharon Blynn (*Soren*), Auden L Ophuls (*Talos' Daughter*), Harriet L Ophuls (*Talos' Daughter*), Reggie (*Goose*), Gonzo (*Goose*), Archie (*Goose*), Rizzo (*Goose*), Chris Evans (*Steve Rogers/Captain America*), Scarlett Johansson (*Natasha Romanoff/Black Widow*), Don Cheadle (*James Rhodes/War Machine*), Mark Ruffalo (*Bruce Banner*)

Having been separated from the rest of her team, Kree warrior Vers winds up on Earth where she meets S.H.I.E.L.D. agent Nick Fury. Together, the pair uncover the truth behind Vers' past and her role in the ongoing conflict between the Kree and the Skrulls.

Captain Marvel is one of the strongest figures in the Marvel Cinematic Universe—not just with her powers but as a symbol of female empowerment. Marvel Studios' first film with a stand-alone female lead was a long time coming.

Captain Marvel was officially announced in October 2014, with a planned release date of 6 July 2018. Given the inclusion of *Spider-Man: Homecoming* to the Phase Three slate, the date would later be moved to 2 November 2018. In April 2015, Nicole Perlman and Meg LeFauve were hired to write the screenplay. (Geneva Robertson-Dworet would take over in August 2017, with LeFauve going on to co-direct *Gigantic*, although the project would be cancelled in October 2017). In October the same year, *Captain Marvel* would be pushed back again, this time to 8 March 2019, to accommodate *Ant-Man and the Wasp*.

Academy Award winner Brie Larson was officially announced as Carol Danvers/Captain Marvel during Marvel Studios' Hall H panel at the 2016 San

Diego Comic-Con. Larson trained for the role over a period of nine months, enlisting trainer Jason Walsh to help her get into shape. In addition to boxing, judo, and wrestling, weightlifting exercises formed an integral part of her routine, with a particular focus on improving her upper body strength.

A female director was sought, with Marvel reportedly looking at Niki Caro, Lesli Linka Glatter, and Lorene Scafaria, though Kevin Feige wanted to refine the story and the script before having further discussions with candidates. In the end, directing duo Anna Boden and Ryan Fleck landed the job. Though Boden and Fleck had previously only worked on indie films, it was their character-driven approach and understanding of Carol that led to their hiring.

Joining Larson would be Samuel L Jackson, reprising his role as Nick Fury. The pair previously worked together on *Kong: Skull Island* (2017) and *Unicorn Store* (2017), the latter being Larson's feature directorial debut. Another returning MCU figure is Phil Coulson, played by Clark Gregg. In 2017, Feige revealed at Marvel's San Diego Comic-Con panel that *Captain Marvel* will take place during the '90s and that the shape-shifting alien Skrulls would feature in the plot. Ben Mendelsohn—who previously worked with Boden and Fleck on *Mississippi Grind* (2015)—was cast as Talos, a leader of the Skrulls, as well as S.H.I.E.L.D. director Keller. Mendelsohn uses an American accent when playing Keller and his native Australian accent when portraying Talos.

Though the character he plays was initially kept a secret from the public, Jude Law was later confirmed to play Yon-Rogg, commander of the Kree Starforce. Other Starforce members include Minn-Erva played by Gemma Chan, Att-Lass played by Algenis Pérez Soto, Bron-Char played by Rune Temte, and Korath, with Djimon Housou reprising the role from *Guardians of the Galaxy* (2014). Lee Pace's *Guardians* villain Ronan also makes an appearance.

Other cast members include Annette Bening as Wendy Lawson, Lashana Lynch as Maria Rambeau (Lynch replaced DeWanda Wise due to scheduling conflicts with *She's Gotta Have It*, 2017-19), and Akira Akbar as Monica Rambeau. Four cats portrayed Goose, a feline-looking alien creature: Archie, Gonzo, Rizzo, and Reggie, who was the primary cat used. Named Chewie in the comics (a nod to Chewbacca from *Star Wars*), the character was renamed Goose after the character of the same name from the 1986 film *Top Gun*, allowing the filmmakers to link the cat to Danvers' past as a US Air Force pilot.

Marvel would later reveal that Liz Flahive and Carly Mensch along with Boden and Fleck made contributions to the screenplay. Though *Avengers: Endgame* would be released after *Captain Marvel*, Larson filmed her scenes on the ensemble film before commencing work on her character's solo movie. Principal photography for *Captain Marvel* officially began in March 2018, although some footage was shot earlier in January 2018. The seventy-five-day shoot concluded on 6 July 2018.

As research, Larson and Boden visited Nellis Air Force Base in Las Vegas, Nevada. Both women rode up in F-16 fighter jets to get first-hand experience of the g-forces pilots face. Additionally, Larson met with Captain Danielle "Kazi" Park and Brigadier General Jeannie M Leavitt—the US Air Force's first female fighter pilot—to inform her performance. Lynch meanwhile went to Luke Air Force Base for her F-16 flight. She also met up with pilots, spending time with "Taboo" and Kristin "Mother" Hubbard, both of whom are also mothers. The Department of Defense and Air Force's cooperation were instrumental to the film, helping secure filming locations and providing planes and other military equipment for the sets. Pilots also served as consultants and many airmen were used as extras on set.

To help sell the film's period setting, the filmmakers had to painstakingly create sets and props that wouldn't be amiss in 1995. To recreate a Blockbuster store, set decorator Lauri Gaffin and her team bought approximately 7,000 VHS tapes from thrift shops and online. Roughly 4,000 were deemed to be suitable and dressed in Blockbuster branding and labelled with films from the '80s. Nineties candy and soda packaging were also recreated and displayed on the set. The initial plan was to have Vers destroy a standee of the movie *The Mask* (1994), mistaking the green-faced character from the film for a Skrull. Permission for its use was denied, so a *True Lies* (1994) one was used instead, with Arnold Schwarzenegger giving his blessing. So convincing was the set (the filmmakers used an abandoned strip mall) that members of the public tried to visit the store, assuming it was a real Blockbuster! For the internet café Vers later visits, production designer Andy Nicholson sourced old computers with blocky monitors from Los Angeles prop companies. Other touches include Vers' Nine Inch Nails shirt (chosen as the logo wasn't too distracting) and the myriad of '90s tracks such as "Only Happy When It Rains" by Garbage and "Come as You Are" by Nirvana.

Captain Marvel had its world premiere at the El Capitan Theatre in Los Angeles on 4 March 2019. Marvel's first female-led film proved to be another hit for the studio, becoming the first female-led superhero movie to make over $1 billion worldwide. Fans appreciated how older elements from Carol Danvers' convoluted history are cleverly interpreted for the screen, with the filmmakers skilfully weaving in elements from more recent story arcs. With a fine start, the *Captain Marvel* franchise can now take off in earnest and go higher from here.

Excelsior!
Stan Lee appears as a passenger on the train, going over the lines for his role in *Mallrats* (1995). Lee wasn't in the best of health (his cameo was shot a few months before his passing) and so couldn't deliver his lines properly. Kevin Feige reached out to *Mallrats* director Kevin Smith, who went on to help him obtain audio from alternate takes of Lee's role in the film.

Mid-Credits Scene
Steve Rogers, Natasha Romanoff, Rhodey, and Bruce Banner find that Nick Fury's pager has stopped working. Steve tells them to send the signal again when Captain Marvel appears, asking where Fury is. *Avengers: Endgame* directors Anthony and Joe Russo filmed the scene. Larson shot her part against green screen, with none of the other actors present.

Post-Credits Scene
Goose sits on Fury's desk, coughing up the Tesseract.

Marvellous Miscellanea
- *Open World* was used as the working title for the film.
- As a tribute to Stan Lee—who passed away on 12 November 2018 while *Captain Marvel* was being edited—the opening Marvel Studios logo features images and footage of his various MCU cameos, as well as behind-the-scenes clips of him interacting with various actors and directors.
- The filmmakers looked at mushroom growth, popcorn popping, snakes shedding their skin, and how octopuses and squids change colour as references for the Skrull transformation process.
- Pancho's Bar is named after Florence Lowe "Pancho" Barnes who, among other achievements, was the first female stunt pilot in motion pictures and founded the Women's Air Reserve.
- Pilots Matthew "Spider" Kimmel and Stephen "Cajun" Del Bagno served as consultants on *Captain Marvel* and make cameo appearances in the film. Del Bagno can be seen playing crud (a variant of billiards played by

military personnel) with Carol Danvers and Maria Rambeau at Pancho's Bar. He sadly passed away during a training mission a week after working on the movie. *Captain Marvel* is dedicated to his memory.

- During the mind frack sequence, when Vers recalls being shot by a Skrull, for a split second its ears appear to be human, an indication of how unreliable her memory is. There's also a quick shot of a burning piano, an activity done by air force pilots as a tribute to a fallen colleague. The tradition supposedly started during World War II when a piano-playing member of the Royal Air Force was killed. Given they would no longer hear their friend play the instrument, his comrades burnt his piano in his memory.
- Given some of the surrealist imagery used, the directors turned to *Eternal Sunshine of the Spotless Mind* (2004) as inspiration for the mind frack sequence.
- As Vers comes out of the mind frack sequence, Anna Boden's son can be seen on the bank of monitors. Additionally, the Skrull that says, "Uh oh," is voiced by Boden. The co-director also supplied the "Uh oh" sound heard when Carol retrieves her boots.
- Barry Curtis, who's been a part of Marvel Studios' security team on several MCU films, plays the mall security guard Carol meets after exiting the Blockbuster.
- To de-age Jackson, Lola Visual Effects primarily used the actor's appearance in *One Eight Seven* (1997) as a reference but also looked at *Die Hard with a Vengeance* (1995) and *National Lampoon's Loaded Weapon 1* (1993).
- *The French Connection* (1971) was used as inspiration for the train chase/fight between Vers and a Skrull. In *The French Connection*, detective Jimmy "Popeye" Doyle spots the person he's after on a subway station. The twist in *Captain Marvel* is that Vers isn't sure who she's after!
- When Vers gets off the train, one of the people she passes is comic book writer Kelly Sue DeConnick (she has red hair and is wearing glasses). Her run on *Captain Marvel* was used as the basis for the film. Soon after, Vers passes a man wearing a blue Los Angeles Dodgers cap and a plaid shirt. That's Ted Yonenaka, a chef on the film and craft service personnel.
- Nick Fury looking at the Skrull's genitals during the autopsy scene was improvised. Later on, when Fury and Vers are talking at Pancho's Bar, Fury says, "I like the B's. I can make them rhyme," a line Jackson suggested he use.

- Brie Larson is severely allergic to cats, and so couldn't be around Reggie for long periods of time.
- The cockpit of the Quadjet is actually a set from the television series *Agents of S.H.I.E.L.D.* (2013-20).
- Talos drinking from a takeaway cup isn't meant to be a reference to *Pulp Fiction* (1994) as many fans assumed, but rather *Reservoir Dogs* (1992).

From Panels to the Screen

Though not a direct adaptation, the general story of the "Kree/Skrull War" (*The Avengers* #89-97, 1971-72) is used as the basis for the film, where the Kree and the Skrulls fight each other with Earth caught in between.

A former US Air Force pilot, the comic book incarnation of Carol Danvers gained her initial powers of flight and enhanced strength after being caught in the explosion of a damaged Kree Psyche-Magnitron. This was amidst a fight between the Kree warriors Mar-Vell/Captain Marvel and Yon-Rogg (*Captain Marvel* #18, 1969). The Psyche-Magnitron—a machine that converts thoughts into reality—alters her genes and turns her into a human/Kree hybrid, granting her the abilities possessed by Mar-Vell. A slight retcon to her origins would occur in *The Life of Captain Marvel* #4 (2018), in which it is revealed that Carol is in fact half Kree, and that the Kree Psyche-Magnitron merely activated her latent powers. Towards the end of the film, Carol finally gains access to all her power. This could be a reference to when her comic book counterpart became Binary. As Binary, Carol could access the power of a white hole, augmenting her strength and enabling her to release heat, light, and various forms of radiation (prior to this she had lost her powers to the mutant Rogue). Notably, her skin turned red and her hair became cosmic flames. Though she eventually losses her connection to the white hole (she did, however, retain her Binary abilities, albeit in a weakened form), she is able to return to this state if she absorbs enough energy. Originally going by the code name "Ms Marvel," Carol would also go on to use the names Binary and Warbird, before taking on the mantle of Captain Marvel in *Captain Marvel* #1 (2012).

In the film, we briefly see Carol's father, Joseph Danvers, and brother, Steve Danvers, though in the comics she has an additional sibling, Joseph Danvers Jr. At one point in the film, Carol says, "Higher, further, faster, baby," a nod to the *Captain Marvel* comic arc titled "Higher, further, faster, more," (*Captain Marvel* #1-6, 2014) as well as being words Carol's mentor, Helen

Cobb, wrote to her to describe their similar mindsets and desire to push boundaries.

While Maria Rambeau is a character taken from the comics, it is her daughter—Monica Rambeau—who is friends with Carol in the source material. A hero in her own right, Monica Rambeau has the ability to convert her body into various types of energy. Monica has also used various code names throughout her career, including Captain Marvel, Pulsar, and Photon (Maria's call sign in the film is a nod to this). Carol affectionately calls Monica "Lieutenant Trouble," which in the comic books is a nickname Carol gives to a young friend and fan, Katherine Renner.

The Air Force not allowing Carol and Maria to fly planes in combat missions bears a resemblance to Helen Cobb's situation from the comics. In 1961, Helen is told that she and her fellow female pilots are not permitted to become astronauts as they lack military jet experience, experience they cannot obtain as women were barred from flying jets.

Early on in the movie, we see Starforce dispatched on a mission to Torfa. The planet is a relatively minor one in the comics, known for its poisonous atmosphere resulting from vibranium extraction. In the comics, Starforce are a group of Kree warriors tasked with protecting the Kree Empire. Formed by the Supreme Intelligence, the initial comic lineup consisted of Att-Lass/Captain Atlas (a soldier trained in many forms of combat), Minn-Erva/Doctor Minerva (a pilot and gifted bio-geneticist; in the film she's Starforce's sniper), Korath the Pursuer (a cyber-geneticist), Shatterax (cybernetically enhanced warrior; not present in the film), Supremor (an android housing the Supreme Intelligence's consciousness; doesn't appear in the film), and Ultimus (has the ability to manipulate cosmic energy; not present in the film).

The comic book incarnation of Bron Char (rendered as Bron-Char in the film) is a member of the Lunatic Legion, a group whose goal is to destroy the human race. Though a scout in the movie, in the comics Soh-Larr was a Kree warrior who fell in love with a Skrull, Ryga'a, with whom he had a child, Dorrek Supreme. Yon-Rogg was a colonel in the Kree army, unlike his cinematic counterpart who is the commander of Starforce. His antagonistic relationship with Mar-Vell from the source material has been carried over to the film.

In the comics, the Supreme Intelligence is an organic computer created by the Kree Science Council, initially designed to help the alien race create a Cosmic Cube. Upon gaining sentience, however, the Supremor refused, knowing the danger such an object posed. Composed of the brightest Kree minds, it served as the leader of the Kree Empire for many years. In the source material, it's depicted as a large, green floating head; its true form in the film, however, has yet to be revealed.

Mar-Vell has been changed from a male to a female for the Marvel Cinematic Universe. The comic book incarnation of Mar-Vell was sent to Earth to spy on humanity. Adopting the identity of Dr Walter Lawson (the name of a scientist Mar-Vell encountered who had passed away; changed to Wendy Lawson in the film), he began working at the Cape Canaveral military base, where he would meet the facility's security chief, Carol Danvers. Mar-Vell would go on to defend humanity many times despite his mission, before dying of cancer as depicted in the graphic novel *The Death of Captain Marvel* (1982).

The aircraft Wendy Lawson designs is called the *Asis*. This is a reference to the Asis program from the Ultimate Universe. Mahr Vehl (the Ultimate Universe version of Mar-Vell) joins the program in an effort to help humanity with interstellar travel.

In both the comic books and the film, Skrulls are a green-skinned, reptilian alien race with the ability to shape-shift. Originating from the planet Skrullos, Skrulls have a warrior culture and, like the Kree, have conquered many worlds throughout the galaxy. Unlike his cinematic counterpart, Talos wasn't born with the ability to shape-shift in the comics. A skilled combatant, parts of his body have been cybernetically enhanced, giving him super strength.

An agent of S.H.I.E.L.D. named Keller exists in the comics, though it's unknown if the film's Keller, the director of S.H.I.E.L.D., is meant to be his MCU equivalent or if the name-sharing is merely a coincidence. Although Nick Fury hails from New York City in the source material, his film counterpart tells Carol that he was born in Huntsville, Alabama. His middle name of Joseph, however, is something both incarnations share. The comic book version of Fury loses the ability to see with his left eye as a result of a grenade blast, whereas his film counterpart has the misfortune of losing it after Goose scratches it.

In the comics, Carol calls her pet Chewie (named after the *Star Wars* character Chewbacca, since Carol is a fan of the franchise), whilst in the movie the cat is named Goose. Both Goose and Chewie aren't real house cats, but rather an alien species known as Flerken (Rocket Raccoon reveals this to Carol in *Captain Marvel* #7, 2014) that look like domestic felines. Flerkens possess tentacles that are released from their mouths, lay eggs to reproduce, and contain pocket dimensions within their bodies.

Some of the costume colours Carol cycles through appear to be references to costumes she's worn in the comics. The red and yellow combination could allude to Carol's original Ms Marvel outfit; the predominantly black one may refer to the costume she first wears in *Ms. Marvel* #20 (1978); and the green and white one is a nod to the classic Kree uniform.

Captain Marvel's pose when confronting the Kree ships, putting her fist into her other hand, is reminiscent of the cover to *Captain Marvel* #1 (2016). Carol's call sign in the MCU is "Avenger," though her comic book counterpart has the decidedly less cool call sign of "Cheeseburger" (she got the name after vomiting during a g-force simulator exercise).

MCU Easter Eggs

Audiences are introduced to younger versions of Korath and Ronan. The space-jumps through honeycomb-shaped portals, known as the Universal Neural Teleportation Network, is a design first established in *Guardians of the Galaxy Vol. 2*. Once again, S.H.I.E.L.D. has a presence in a Marvel movie. We see an early version of Project Pegasus, the facility where it's based making appearances in *Thor* (2011) and *The Avengers* (2012), and in turn, the Tesseract is seen on-screen once again. At one point, Carol Danvers flies a Quadjet, a precursor to the Quinjet. Carol gives Fury a modified pager to contact her, a device we see him use at the end of *Avengers: Infinity War*. Fury puts into motion his "Avenger Initiative," originally naming it the "Protector Initiative." Lastly, for the mid-credits scene, we get a sequence depicting Steve Rogers, Natasha Romanoff, Bruce Banner, and James Rhodes monitoring the pager, culminating in Carol's arrival back on Earth, which leads into *Avengers: Endgame*.

Chopped, Changed, and Lengthened

- In *The Empire Film Podcast* spoiler special for *Captain Marvel*, Ryan Fleck revealed that an early iteration of the script opened with Carol Danvers and Maria Rambeau in their planes during a combat simulation. The film would have jumped to the present, showing Captain Marvel on another planet, before exploring how she went from being a pilot to becoming a superhero. The idea was abandoned as the filmmakers felt it was more effective for Carol to discover her past along with the audience.
- In an interview with NME, Ben Mendelsohn revealed that a version of the script saw Talos killed partway through the film.

- Yon-Rogg teaches a class of young Kree about the Kree-Skrull war, with Vers subsequently telling the students about how the Skrulls took her family and memory away from her but that the Supreme Intelligence granted her powers to combat them. Yon-Rogg dismisses the class before we cut to him and Vers sparring.
- We see the Starforce team bantering amongst themselves on their ship before prepping to be dispatched to Torfa.
- Yon-Rogg convenes with the Supreme Intelligence, who he sees as an older version of himself. The Supreme Intelligence details how Yon-Rogg has failed in the past and tasks him with bringing the core and Vers back to Hala alive.
- Vers' encounter with the motorcyclist was originally longer. The man asks Vers if she needs a ride, before asking her to smile for him. She offers him a handshake instead, introducing herself. Carol, still holding onto the man's hand, gives him a jolt. She tells him to hand over his jacket, helmet, and motorcycle in exchange for his hand back, to which he obliges.
- Taking place after the Skrull autopsy, Agent Coulson encounters Keller trying to get into his office. Keller claims to have forgotten his badge and Coulson uses his to give Keller access. Inside, Keller—Talos in disguise—goes up to the body of the real Keller, who's tied up, and takes his badge.
- At the Project Pegasus facility, a technician tells Keller that it will take time for the Quadjet to be located. A woman comes up to him and hands him a file on the crash Vers and Wendy Lawson were involved in.
- Carol is conversing with the Supreme Intelligence (who appears as Mar-Vell). She tells it that she knows the implant isn't the source of her power and that it's used to control her. Carol disables the chip and fires blasts at the Intelligence. The Supreme Intelligence then reveals its true form—a large green head—before ending the communication.
- Originally, the film's ending included Carol flying off into space by herself. Editor Debbie Berman felt the ending could be stronger and more meaningful. As such, the scene was adjusted to show Talos and the other Skrulls waiting for her and subsequently heading off together.

Location, Location

A beach on the shores of Shaver Lake in California was transformed into the **crash site** of Wendy Lawson's aircraft. Eagle Rock Substation (7888 N

Figueroa Street, Los Angeles, California) was used as the **Kree training room** where Yon-Rogg and Vers spar. For **Torfa**, the filmmakers used PW Gillibrand Quarry (5810 Bennett Road, Simi Valley, California). That's Hangar 1600 of **Edwards Air Force Base** we see in Vers' memory, a location previously used in *Iron Man* (2008). The now-closed Jim Hall Racing Club (2600 Challenger Place, Oxnard, California) was used as the **go-kart track** young Carol Danvers rides on. The filmmakers used Fulcrum Adventures, located in Culver City Park (9910 Jefferson Boulevard, Culver City, California), for the **ropes course** Carol traverses.

Escaping the Skrulls, Vers lands on Earth, crashing through a **Blockbuster**. The empty shop at 6321 Laurel Canyon Boulevard in North Hollywood, California, was used, including its parking lot when Vers exits. Vers uses a payphone next to the **Slow Club** to contact Yon-Rogg, with the filmmakers dressing the building on the corner of Vantage Avenue and Sylvan Street. The **beach** where Talos and his men land is El Segundo Beach, which is situated next to an oil refinery. Vers chases a Skrull disguised as a surfer to **Douglas Station** in El Segundo, California. **Chasing after the train**, Fury drives west on E Maple Avenue before turning right onto N Nash Street. After the shot of Vers chasing after the Skrull on top of the train, we see Fury heading north on N Nash Street before turning onto Atwood Way. When we see him **swerving through traffic** (just before "Coulson" informs him that the train is going to go into a tunnel), Fury is heading east on E 1st Street (between S Clarence Street and S Gless Street). Digital trickery is used to make it appear as if the train tracks lead down from the bridge and onto street level. The **tunnel** the train heads into is on E 1st Street, between S Gless Street and S Pecan Street. Trying to beat the train to the station, Fury's car leaps out of Lebanon Street, crossing through the Wilshire Boulevard intersection, before continuing down the road. **Fury fights the Coulson impersonator** as they travel down W Temple Street (between N Broadway and N Spring Street), before crashing into a bus and stopping on N Hill Street, outside the Kenneth Hahn Hall of Administration (500 W Temple Street, Los Angeles). **Vers gets off the train** at 7th Street/Metro Center Station but, thanks to the magic of editing, actually exits out of Civic Center/Grand Park Station (taking the exit leading to N Hill Street).

The **internet café** Vers visits to conduct some research is a retail space that can be found at 1404 W 6th Street, Los Angeles. After stealing a motorbike, she rides out of the shopping area and heads south down **Valencia**

Street. Zebra stands in for the exterior of **Pancho's Bar** but is actually a strip club located at 2763 Sierra Highway, Rosamond, California. The interior was shot at Tinhorn Flats Saloon & Grill (2623 W Magnolia Boulevard, Burbank, California). The entrance to the **Project Pegasus facility** was filmed near California's Pyramid Lake, with the tunnel Fury and Vers drive down being part of Eastwood Powerhouse. For the hangar, the filmmakers used Edwards Air Force Base, while the facility's records room was filmed at the University of California, Los Angeles Southern Regional Library Facility basement (305 De Neve Drive, Los Angeles).

A plantation house outside of Baton Rouge, Louisiana, was used as **Maria Rambeau's residence**. We see more flashbacks as Captain Marvel convenes with the Supreme Intelligence. The shot of a **young Carol falling off her bike** was filmed in a Culver City Park parking lot, north west of Bill Botts Field (also referred to as the Lower Field). In fact, the field itself is used in the film as the location for the scene of **young Carol playing baseball**. The **desert** where Yon-Rogg crashes and has his final confrontation with Captain Marvel was filmed in the Lucerne Valley area of the Mojave Desert.

AVENGERS: ENDGAME

Directors: Anthony and Joe Russo
Screenplay: Christopher Markus & Stephen McFeely

Producer: Kevin Feige
Executive Producers: Louis D'Esposito, Victoria Alonso, Michael Grillo, Trinh Tran, Jon Favreau, James Gunn, and Stan Lee
Co-Producers: Mitch Bell, Christopher Markus, Stephen McFeely, and Jen Underdahl
Associate Producers: JoAnn Perritano and Ari Costa

Cinematography: Trent Opaloch
Production Design: Charles Wood
Editing: Jeffrey Ford and Matthew Schmidt
Music: Alan Silvestri
Costume Design: Judianna Makovsky
Visual Effects Supervisor: Dan Deleeuw
Casting: Sarah Halley Finn

Production Company: Marvel Studios
Distribution Company: Walt Disney Studios Motion Pictures

US Release Date: 26 April 2019
Running Time: 181 minutes
Budget: $356 million
Box Office: $2,797,800,564

Based on the Marvel Comics by Stan Lee and Jack Kirby

Cast: Robert Downey Jr (*Tony Stark/Iron Man*), Chris Evans (*Steve Rogers/Captain America*), Mark Ruffalo (*Bruce Banner/Hulk*), Chris Hemsworth (*Thor*), Scarlett Johansson (*Natasha Romanoff/Black Widow*), Jeremy Renner (*Clint Barton/Hawkeye*), Don Cheadle (*James Rhodes/War Machine*), Paul Rudd (*Scott Lang/Ant-Man*), Benedict Cumberbatch (*Doctor Strange*), Chadwick Boseman (*T'Challa/Black Panther*), Brie Larson (*Carol Danvers/Captain Marvel*), Tom Holland (*Peter Parker/Spider-Man*), Karen Gillan (*Nebula*), Zoe Saldana (*Gamora*), Evangeline Lilly (*Hope van Dyne/Wasp*), Tessa Thompson (*Valkyrie*), Rene Russo (*Frigga*), Elizabeth Olsen (*Wanda Maximoff/Scarlet Witch*), Anthony Mackie (*Sam Wilson/Falcon*), Sebastian Stan (*Bucky Barnes/Winter Soldier*), Tom Hiddleston (*Loki*), Danai Gurira (*Okoye*), Benedict Wong (*Wong*), Pom Klementieff (*Mantis*), Dave Bautista (*Drax*), Letitia Wright (*Shuri*), John Slattery (*Howard Stark*), Tilda Swinton (*The Ancient One*), Jon Favreau (*Happy Hogan*), Hayley Atwell (*Peggy Carter*), Natalie Portman (*Jane Foster*), Marisa Tomei (*Aunt May*), Taika Waititi (*Korg*), Angela Bassett (*Ramonda*), Michael Douglas (*Hank Pym*), Michelle Pfeiffer (*Janet van Dyne*), William Hurt (*Secretary of State Thaddeus Ross*), Cobie Smulders (*Maria Hill*), Sean Gunn (*On-Set Rocket* and *Kraglin*), Winston Duke (*M'Baku*), Linda Cardellini (*Laura Barton*), Maximiliano Hernandez (*Agent Sitwell*), Frank Grillo (*Brock Rumlow*), Hiroyuki Sanada (*Akihiko*), Tom Vaughan-Lawlor (*Ebony Maw*), James D'Arcy (*Jarvis*), Jacob Batalon (*Ned*), Vin Diesel (*Groot*), Bradley Cooper (*Rocket*), Gwyneth Paltrow (*Pepper Potts*), Robert Redford (*Alexander Pierce*), Josh Brolin (*Thanos*), Chris Pratt (*Peter Quill/Star-Lord*), Samuel L Jackson (*Nick Fury*), Lexi Rabe (*Morgan Stark*), Ross Marquand (*Red Skull (Stonekeeper)*), Gozie Agbo (*Grieving Man*), Emma Fuhrmann (*Cassie Lang*), Michael Shaw (*Corvus Glaive*), Terry Notary (*On-Set Groot* and *Cull Obsidian*), Kerry Condon (*FRIDAY*), Ben Sakamoto (*Cooper Barton*), Ava Russo (*Lila Barton*), Cade Woodward (*Nathaniel Barton*), Stan Lee (*Driver*), Yvette Nicole Brown (*S.H.I.E.L.D. Agent*), Callan Mulvey (*Jack Rollins*), Lia Russo (*Lia*), Julian Russo (*Julian*), Taylor Patterson (*Taylor*), Agostino Rosalina (*Augie*), Ken Jeong (*Security Guard*), Ty Simpkins (*Harley Keener*), Jackson Dunn (*Scott Lang (12 Years Old)*), Lee Moore (*Scott Lang (93 Years Old)*), Bazlo LeClair (*Scott Lang (Baby)*), Loen LeClair (*Scott Lang (Baby)*), Matthew Berry (*S.H.I.E.L.D. Agent*), Jim Starlin (*Support Group Man #1*), Jimmy Ray Pickens (*Support Group Man #2*), Jack Champion (*Kid on Bike*)

After failing to stop Thanos from wiping out half of the universe's inhabitants, the remaining Avengers find they have another chance to bring back all that they've lost.

Avengers: Infinity War ended with the Avengers defeated and Thanos the victor. Audiences were stunned. With the heroes in such a dire place, how would they continue after what Thanos had done?

The bulk of the filming for the next *Avengers* film began on 10 August 2017 and wrapped on 11 January 2018. No longer called *Avengers: Infinity War – Part II*, the film's title—*Avengers: Endgame*—wouldn't be revealed until the release of the first trailer on 7 December 2018.

With the fourth *Avengers* film not being based on any particular story from the comics, audiences were in for some surprises. The first big twist in fact occurs twenty minutes into the film, with Thor chopping Thanos' head off. The idea to get rid of the film's antagonist came from executive producer Trinh Tran who suggested it after the filmmakers were unsure of what to do with the character. The next twist would come soon after, with the narrative skipping ahead five years. This enabled the full extent of what Thanos did to be shown and explore how all the people who were left have coped.

It was decided that *Endgame* would feature time travel, a natural plot device given the Quantum Realm had already been introduced in the *Ant-Man* films. Physicists were consulted, who explained that the mechanics of time travel most people know—going into the past will change aspects of the future—isn't what they believe to be correct. Instead, they believe that altering the past results in an alternate timeline or reality being created, branching off at the point of change.

With this model in place, the filmmakers then had to decide which points in the MCU history the heroes would revisit. Writers Christopher Markus and Stephen McFeely compiled a list of the Infinity Stones, detailing where they had been and the years they were there. From this, locations and time periods were chosen based on what stories they thought they could tell with certain characters. Originally, the writers felt revisiting the Battle of New York would be pandering to audiences and avoided it in the first draft of the screenplay. Rather, they had characters go to Asgard to retrieve the Tesseract and the Aether. Iron Man would have used a stealth suit, rendering him invisible, but would still have been seen by Heimdall, the pair subsequently fighting. The same iteration of the script also saw War Machine, Nebula, Black Widow, and Hawkeye visiting the temple on Morag while it was still submerged under water. This latter scenario complicated matters, as it didn't allow Thanos to catch on to the fact that someone was after the Power Stone, and so the time period was changed to Morag in 2014 so the writers could bring the past versions of Thanos, Gamora, and Nebula into the story. It was co-director Joe Russo who ultimately convinced Markus and McFeely to use the 2012 New York setting.

The Avengers' quest to obtain the Infinity Stones wouldn't be without loss, with Black Widow sacrificing herself in exchange for the Soul Stone. The decision wasn't made lightly given Natasha Romanoff is the only female of the founding six members. A version was written in which Hawkeye made the sacrifice instead. Upon reading this, however, visual effects producer Jen Underdahl convinced the writers otherwise, arguing that this allowed Natasha's arc to be completed.

While it's the original six Avengers, Ant-Man, War Machine, and remaining Guardians of the Galaxy members Rocket and Nebula that feature in the main story, several actors from previous MCU films reprise their roles despite the deaths of their respective characters. These include Tilda Swinton as the Ancient One, Rene Russo as Frigga, and John Slattery as Howard Stark. And despite announcing *The Old Man & the Gun* (2018) to be his final acting performance before retiring, Robert Redford appears in *Endgame* as Alexander Pierce. Arguably the biggest surprise though would be the return of all the heroes who were snapped away, arriving through portals to battle Thanos and his forces.

The reveal of the characters arriving through the portals was originally a much quicker sequence, with the heroes stepping through simultaneously. It was reshot with the arrivals staggered and to feature each character properly. Given the enormity of the sequence, some hero groupings had to be compiled from multiple shots for logistical reasons or due to actors' schedules. While Dave Bautista and Pom Klementieff were filmed together exiting the portal from Titan, Benedict Cumberbatch was filmed separately to show Doctor Strange flying in with them. Chris Pratt and Tom Holland were shot separately on different days given their availability. Though not seen in the subsequent battle, Howard the Duck walking out of a portal from Contraxia was actually a late inclusion requested by the filmmakers. Weta Digital created and animated the character, inserting him in between some Ravagers. All in all, Howard appears on screen for eighteen frames.

With *Endgame*, Tony Stark ensures the one reality in which they successfully defeat Thanos occurs by using the six Infinity Stones, resulting in his death. Originally, Tony didn't say a word to Thanos as he snaps his fingers, though Robert Downey Jr was also filmed improvising lines. Finding that none of the options filmed were working, editor Jeffrey Ford suggested

Tony say, "I am Iron Man," in response to Thanos' "I am inevitable." Robert Downey Jr was hesitant to reshoot the moment, not wanting to get back into the emotional space, but was convinced to do so by friend Joel Silver. The now-iconic moment was shot during reshoots, filmed on a stage that was next door to the one in which Downey filmed his audition for Tony Stark.

Tony's funeral was just as star-studded as the final battle. To preserve the secrecy of what was being filmed, many actors were told they were shooting a wedding, only finding out on the day of the shoot the true nature of the scene. Given her role, Gwyneth Paltrow was one of the few actors told beforehand. The scene was shot on 7 October 2017—the same day a group photo was taken to mark Marvel Studios' tenth anniversary.

Steve Rogers was also given an ending, the character going back in time to live out his life with Peggy Carter. In a way, Steve and Tony have swapped roles: Tony makes the ultimate sacrifice while Steve pursues a self-interest. The scene that features old Steve was filmed with Chris Evans playing his aged character (wearing a wig and wrinkle prosthetics applied around his eyes and on his neck), as well as an elderly stand-in, Patrick Gorman, to give the visual effects team a reference for the character's skin. While the character was around 119 years old, it was decided to give Steve the appearance of a man in his eighties or nineties, befitting his enhanced body. Lola Visual Effects were assigned to digitally age Steve. As Evans had worn some old-age makeup for the scene—which was filmed before the design of elderly-looking Steve was finalised—Lola had to digitally remove the wrinkles from his face before digitally aging the character. Wrinkles were added to Steve, his neck and shoulders were shrunk, and his nose enlarged among other aging effects. Steve's voice was provided by Evans himself and was unaltered, the actor merely adjusting his voice to sound older.

On 22 April 2019, *Avengers: Endgame* had its world premiere at the Los Angeles Convention Center. A culmination of the twenty-one films that preceded it, both critics and audiences found *Endgame* to be visually epic and emotionally satisfying. During the course of its run, it obliterated many worldwide box office records including the highest opening weekend gross and the fastest film to make $2 billion (doing so in eleven days). Eventually—with the help of a re-release in June that added a Stan Lee tribute, a deleted scene, and the opening scene to *Spider-Man: Far From Home*, all at the end of the film—it managed to overtake *Avatar* (2009) as the highest grossing movie of all time. With a large scope that celebrates the Marvel Cinematic Universe, *Avengers: Endgame* is both a fulfilling journey and a wonderful end.

Excelsior!

A digitally de-aged Stan Lee drives past Camp Lehigh Army Base, shouting, "Hey, man! Make love, not war."

Marvellous Miscellanea

- The title of the movie was *Avengers: Infinity Gauntlet* before the filmmakers settled on *Avengers: Endgame*.
- The opening scene at Clint Barton's home was originally a part of *Avengers: Infinity War* and would have been shown after Thanos "snaps" away half of all life in the universe. The filmmakers found that it didn't quite work when cut together and so moved it to *Endgame* instead.
- Ingeniously, the Marvel Studios logo omits characters that have disappeared as a result of the Snap.
- The costume Captain Marvel wears in *Endgame* was actually meant to be the same red, blue, and gold-coloured costume she wears in her solo film. The filmmakers decided to give the character new outfits (one for scenes set before the five year jump and a different one for after), and so they digitally replaced the physical costume Larson wore during shooting in post-production.
- In order to prevent any potential leaks and spoilers, a fake scene was written in which Thanos, instead of being decapitated by Thor, is knocked unconscious.
- Co-director Joe Russo makes another appearance in an MCU film, this time appearing as a participant in Steve Rogers' survivors' support group. Notably, he plays the first openly gay character in an MCU film. Also present at the meeting is comic book writer and artist Jim Starlin, the creator of Thanos.
- In the support group scene is a sign that says, "For God and Country: In Memorial to Chaplain Matthew Haggerty." Haggerty was a second assistant director on *Infinity War* and *Endgame*. The names of other staff members can be seen on the Vanished Memorial. These include Dan Deleeuw (visual effects supervisor), Emily Denker (lead VFX editor), Federico Dominguez (VFX line producer: DNEG), and Hannah Long (VFX editor).
- Two actors from the sitcom *Community* (2009-15) make cameo appearances. Ken Jeong portrays the security guard at the U-Store-It facility, while Yvette Nicole Brown is the S.H.I.E.L.D. agent who's in the lift with Tony and Steve at Camp Lehigh Army Base.

- Joe Russo's two youngest daughters make appearances in the film: Ava Russo portrays Lila Barton, while Lia Russo can be seen in the diner, asking for a picture with the Hulk. The other two children in that scene are Julian Russo (Anthony Russo's son) and Agostino "Augie" Rosalina (Anthony and Joe's nephew). Given the school schedules of the three children, their cameos were one of the hardest to organise. Joe's two eldest children also cameo. Scott Lang passes Joe's son, Basil, as he starts to find Cassie's name at the memorial to the Vanished, while Joe's eldest daughter, Sophia, and her boyfriend are the couple Scott moves in front of soon after.
- Originally, when Tony says to Morgan, "Love you tons," she was to reply with the same phrase. However, Robert Downey Jr revealed that in real life his children reply with "I love you 3,000," and so the phrase was incorporated into the film.
- To portray an overweight Thor, Chris Hemsworth wore a sixty-eight-pound (thirty-one-kilogram) fat suit and had dental plumpers inserted into his mouth to make his cheeks appear chubbier.
- Korg can be seen wearing a shirt with pineapples on it—an item of clothing Taika Waititi actually owns.
- All the time suits seen in the film were created with CGI.
- When the Avengers place their fists in the centre of a team huddle before they travel back in time, the red of their gloves and the circular pattern of the quantum tunnel they're standing on evokes the image of Tony's circular arc reactor.
- Despite not filming the third and fourth *Avengers* films simultaneously, scenes using Durham Castle as Asgard were shot during the *Avengers: Infinity War* production schedule.
- While Natalie Portman appears in the film via repurposed deleted footage from *Thor: The Dark World* (2013), she did record new lines specifically for *Endgame*.
- Fantasy sports analyst Matthew Berry appears in the film as a S.H.I.E.L.D. agent. He can be seen next to Alexander Pierce and is the one who tries to take the Tesseract case from Tony.
- Writer Christopher Markus has a cameo in the film. He's the man dressed in a brown suit entering the bunker at Camp Lehigh Army Base.
- Lola Visual Effects used Michael Douglas' appearance in the television show *The Streets of San Francisco* (1972-77) as a reference to de-age the actor.

- Howard Stark is bringing his wife, Maria, sauerkraut as it was something co-writer Stephen McFeely's mother craved when she was pregnant with him.
- The worldwide creative director of Epic Games, Donald Mustard, plays a sorcerer in the film. He can be spotted behind Doctor Strange when Iron Man asks him if this is the one out of 14,000,605 futures in which they win.
- When Tony transfers the Infinity Stones from Thanos to himself, the music that plays is a segment from the track "One Way Trip" that was used in *The Avengers* (2012). In that film, the theme was used when Iron Man carries the missile into the wormhole.
- The Chitauri Leviathan that turns to dust as it's about to swallow Rocket is reminiscent of the moment from *Back to the Future Part II* (1989) when a holographic shark attacks Marty McFly.
- The filmmakers considered digitally inserting Cassie Lang into the crowd at Tony Stark's funeral but decided against it to keep the focus on the heroes commemorating Tony.
- The directors and writers have differing views on the film's ending. The Russo brothers believe that when Steve went back in time to live with Peggy, he did so in an alternate reality. Markus and McFeely, however, think that Steve went back and lived with Peggy in the prime reality, meaning that two Steve Rogers existed at the same time.
- Kevin Feige came up with the idea to give the original six Avengers curtain call endings. He was inspired by the credits to *Star Trek VI: The Undiscovered Country* (1991), which featured the signatures of the cast to the original series, with the *Star Trek* film being the last to feature them all.
- Despite its critical and financial success and a campaign by Disney, *Avengers: Endgame* was only nominated for the Best Visual Effects award at the 92nd Academy Awards.

From Panels to the Screen

Though *Endgame* isn't a direct adaption of any particular comic book storyline, the concept of the Avengers travelling through time is present in the "Avengers Forever" arc (*Avengers Forever* #1-12, 1998-99). In this limited series, various Avengers from the past, present, and future come together to protect Rick Jones from Immortus, the Master of Time. Interestingly, in

Avengers Forever #3 (1999) Kang states, "Time-travel does not change the past—as I trust you've learned. If one alters the flow of events, it merely creates a new, divergent branch of the timestream, while the old one flows on."

Endgame opens with Clint Barton teaching his daughter, Lila, archery. At one point he calls her Hawkeye. There has in fact been a female Hawkeye in the comics, Kate Bishop, who is mentored by Clint. After losing his family to the Snap, Clint takes on a new costume, which harkens to his Ronin identity from the source material. The original Ronin in the comics is Maya Lopez, a deaf woman with photographic reflexes who initially used the name Echo. In a flashback from *The New Avengers* #30 (2007), we see Clint Barton—having given up his identity as Hawkeye—wear Maya's costume and take on the Ronin persona to go on a mission to rescue Maya from the Hand in Japan. It is the Ultimate Universe incarnation of the character, however, who loses his wife and three children (in this instance they were murdered by a black ops team led by Black Widow).

Having rescued Tony Stark, Carol Danvers mentions that she'll bring him a Xorrian elixir. In the comics, the Xorrians (also known as the Xorri) are an ancient humanoid race that spawned other humanoid races such as humans, the Kree, and the Skrulls.

Five years after meeting the Avengers, we see Captain Marvel sporting a short haircut, a look taken from her comic book counterpart. She's also wearing a new outfit, with the design—blue shoulders and gloves, gold star, and red torso and upper thighs—echoing Mar-Vell's most well-known costume from the source material. Black Widow tracks Clint to Japan, locating him just as he kills Akihiko. A version of Akihiko also exists in the comics and is a member of the Yakuza as well.

The introduction of a smart Hulk has a precedent in the source material. First off, there's the Gray Hulk (also known as Joe Fixit), who, while not as smart as Bruce Banner, did have a higher intellect than the green Savage Hulk. Then there's Maestro, an intelligent—but insane—Hulk from Earth-9200. The film, however, seems to have adapted the Merged Hulk (also known as the Professor), who possesses Bruce Banner's intellect and the Savage Hulk's superhuman strength.

The blue and red suit we see Rocket wear in the film is his classic outfit from the comic books. In the film, it's revealed that Thor has established New Asgard in Norway. This has been adapted from *Thor* #2 (2007), with Thor rebuilding Asgard on Earth (floating over Oklahoma) after it's destroyed.

Rhodey brings up the idea of killing baby Thanos so as to not have him grow up and collect the Infinity Stones. A similar idea is played out in *Cosmic Ghost Rider* #1 (2018) with Frank Castle from an alternate reality, who has gained the powers of a Ghost Rider as well as the Power Cosmic, going back in time intending to kill baby Thanos before Thanos becomes evil.

The *Avengers: Endgame* script identifies Korbinites as the soldiers fought by the 2014 versions of Nebula and Gamora. In the comics, Korbinites are a semi-humanoid race with light orange skin that hail from the planet Korbin.

Steve Rogers says, "Hail Hydra," as part of a ruse in the film, with his comic book counterpart uttering the same phrase at the end of *Captain America: Steve Rogers* #1 (2016) (though it would transpire that this Hydra-affiliated version of Captain America is not the classic Cap we all know). The character's new uniform in the film is an adaptation of his classic chain mail costume from the source material.

The Mark 85 Iron Man armour, with the red torso section and gold-coloured arms and legs, evokes the character's early armour models from the source material. For much of the character's history, Tony Stark's limbs appeared to be covered with form fitting sleeves instead of actual armour.

When Black Widow and Hawkeye arrive on Vormir, the Red Skull notes that Natasha's father is named Ivan and Clint's mother is named Edith; this is also true for their comic book counterparts.

When infiltrating Camp Lehigh, Steve wears a uniform bearing the name "Roscoe." In the comics, Roscoe Simons took on the role of Captain America after Steve became Nomad. In Hank Pym's lab, the original Ant-Man helmet from the comics can be seen. In the film, Peggy Carter has a conversation with a S.H.I.E.L.D. agent about someone named Braddock. This could be a reference to the comic book character Brian Braddock who, after getting into a motorcycle accident, is saved by Merlyn and Roma, who transform him into Captain Britain. It could also refer to Brian's father, Sir James Braddock, who was also a member of the Captain Britain Corps. The man who drives Howard Stark is Edwin Jarvis, Howard's butler, and later Tony's, from the comics. The character is played by James D'Arcy who also portrayed him in the *Agent Carter* (2015-16) television series, making this the first time a character from a Marvel Cinematic Universe TV show has appeared in an MCU film.

The Hulk holding up the rubble of the Avengers facility is reminiscent of the character doing a similar act to save his fellow heroes from being crushed under tons of rock in *Secret Wars* #4 (1984). Thanos breaking Captain America's shield occurs in both media, doing so in *The Infinity Gauntlet* #4

(1991). The comic book incarnation of Captain America is also deemed to be worthy enough to wield Mjolnir, first performing this feat in *Thor* #390 (1988). We finally hear the phrase "Avengers assemble!", the team's rallying cry from the source material. It first saw print in *The Avengers* #10 (1964), shouted by Thor. However, *Avengers: Earth's Mightiest Heroes* #4 (2004)—which revisits the events of *The Avengers* #8 (1964)—depicts Captain America uttering the phrase during the Avengers' battle with Kang, canonically making Cap the first to use the battle cry. Pepper Potts' armour reflects how the character gets a suit of her own in the comics, adopting the alias of Rescue. The Rescue armour of the comic books is, as the name suggests, designed for rescue and recovery, possessing no weaponry.

While the Earth-616 incarnation of the Hulk has yet to wield the Infinity Gauntlet, his Ultimate Universe counterpart has, occurring in *Ultimate Comics The Ultimates* #25 (2013). In the Ultimate Universe there are eight Infinity Gems and two Gauntlets (with a space for four gems on each). The Hulk was in possession of both Gauntlets but only five of the gems. Iron Man using the Infinity Gauntlet has also occurred in the comic books, the character doing so in *The Avengers* #12 (2011). In the issue, Iron Man uses it to send the Hood back to prison and then pretends to will the Gauntlet and Infinity Gems to no longer exist (in actuality he wished for the Gauntlet to be transported away, later dividing the Infinity Gems among the Illuminati).

Thor joins the Guardians of the Galaxy, dubbing them the Asgardians of the Galaxy. This is the actual name of a team from the comic books comprising of Annabelle Riggs, Thor's half-sister Angela, Kid Loki, Thunderstrike, Skurge, Valkyrie, and Throg. In both media, Sam Wilson has indeed taken up the mantle of Captain America, with the comic book incarnation first doing so in *Captain America* #25 (2014). Interestingly in both cases, it's an elderly-looking Steve Rogers who appoints his successor.

MCU Easter Eggs

2012 Cap says to his future self, "I can do this all day." Erik Selvig and Sharon Carter are among those that vanished when Thanos used the Infinity Gauntlet. Minor characters reappearing include Jack Rollins (appeared in 2014's *Captain America: The Winter Soldier*), Howard the Duck (first appeared in 2014's *Guardians of the Galaxy*), and Harley Keener (appeared in 2013's *Iron Man 3*). We also see characters on-screen again that have passed away such as Frigga (died in *Thor: The Dark World*), Howard Stark (death seen in *Captain America: Civil War*), the Ancient One (died in *Doctor Strange*), Peggy Carter (died in *Captain America: Civil War*), Agent Sitwell (died in *Captain America: The Winter Soldier*), Brock Rumlow (died in *Captain America: Civil War*), and Alexander Pierce (died in *Captain America: The Winter Soldier*). While on the phone with Alexander Pierce, Agent Sitwell name-drops Dr List, and later on Arnim Zola is mentioned by Howard Stark (while it's almost impossible to see, visual effects studio Cinesite did include a digitized version of Zola's face on a distant screen in the Camp Lehigh underground archive).

Given the numerous callbacks to past films in *Endgame*, those that hark back to a specific film have been categorised as such.

Iron Man – Tony tells Pepper to not post his recording onto social media, recalling the time he told a soldier to not post a picture of the two of them on Myspace. Iron Man's last words are "And I…am…Iron Man." Tony's first arc reactor is seen at his funeral. Morgan shares her father's affinity for cheeseburgers. While *Avengers: Endgame* doesn't have a post-credits scene, the sound of metal being hammered can be heard over the concluding Marvel Studios logo, recalling the scene where Tony Stark builds his first Iron Man armour while in captivity.

Captain America: The First Avenger – Before Steve embarks to return the Infinity Stones, he tells Bucky, "Don't do anything stupid till I get back," with Bucky replying, "How can I? You're taking all the stupid with you." The pair had the same exchange in *Captain America: The First Avenger* (2011), albeit with Bucky saying the first line and Steve replying. At the end of *Endgame*, Steve dances with Peggy, fulfilling a promise he made to her before he became frozen in ice.

The Avengers – Iron Man, Captain America, the Hulk, and Ant-Man revisit the 2012 Battle of New York. On their way to Vormir, Hawkeye remarks to Black Widow that they're "a long way from Budapest," an event first mentioned in *The Avengers*. As they fight the past version of Thanos, Thor charges Iron Man's armour with lightning.

Iron Man 3 – Rhodey's new armour has a red and blue colour scheme, harking back to his Iron Patriot armour.

Thor: The Dark World – Thor and Rocket visit Jane Foster on Asgard in 2013.

Thor tries to explain the colour discrepancy between his eyes to his mother as a result of being hit in the face with a broadsword during the Battle of Harokin, a battle that we first heard about in *The Dark World* (Thor mentions it during a conversation with Sif).

Captain America: The Winter Soldier – Captain America finds himself in an elevator full of S.H.I.E.L.D. agents who are in fact members of Hydra. Before he exits out of a portal, Falcon says to Cap, "On your left," which is what Steve said to Sam every time he passed him during a morning run. The song Peggy and Steve dance to is "It's Been a Long, Long Time" which was played by Nick Fury while he was in Steve's apartment.

Guardians of the Galaxy – On Morag in 2014, Black Widow kicks an orloni just as Peter Quill had done to several of the creatures in the *Guardians of the Galaxy* title sequence. War Machine and Nebula steal the Power Stone before Quill is able to.

Avengers: Age of Ultron – When Steve pays Natasha a visit at the Avengers facility, a pair of ballet shoes can be spotted on a chair, a nod to Natasha's ballet training. Tony and Pepper live on an eco-compound, which was foreshadowed towards the end of *Avengers: Age of Ultron* (2015) when Tony wonders whether he should build Pepper a farm. Captain America finally wields Mjolnir.

Captain America: Civil War – When Clint Barton returns from the time travel test run, Scott Lang runs towards him holding orange slices, a treat Scott asked for after the airport fight. Black Panther calls Clint by his name during the final battle, despite asserting that he didn't care about his name when they first met. Captain America refers to Spider-Man as "Queens" during the final battle.

Spider-Man: Homecoming – Tony gives Peter Parker a hug, having denied him one at the beginning of *Homecoming*. During the final battle, Spider-Man activates his suit's instant kill mode.

Ant-Man and the Wasp – Hope refers to Captain America as "Cap" despite previously making fun of Scott for doing so.

Avengers: Infinity War – Thor kills Thanos by chopping off his head, with Thanos having told him he "should have gone for the head" when attacked by Thor in the previous *Avengers* film. When Rocket talks about the Power Stone, Hulk can be seen eating Ben & Jerry's Hunka Hulka Burnin' Fudge flavoured ice cream (Bruce Banner having learnt the existence of the flavour from Wong in *Infinity War*).

Chopped, Changed, and Lengthened
- An early draft of the script had Black Widow leading an organisation in Washington DC that looked after children orphaned as a result of the Snap.
- A scene of Bruce Banner working in a lab to merge his personality with the Hulk's was written, but ultimately the explanation was conveyed through dialogue in the diner scene instead.
- An early idea the writers had was having Rhodey become vice president sometime in the five years since Thanos snapped away half of all life.
- The filmmakers also considered having War Machine participate in the fight in Edinburgh. During the battle, a member of the Black Order would have sliced the suit in half, before cutting to a scene revealing that Rhodey was piloting the armour remotely. The scene repeated a similar moment from *Iron Man 3* and also brought up the issue of why Rhodey would ever need to be in the suit if he could control it remotely, leading to its omission.
- Other alternate time heist sequences written include the Avengers obtaining the Tesseract from the Triskelion and having someone drive to the Sanctum Sanctorum to retrieve the Time Stone from Doctor Strange.
- A scene was written, but not shot, in which Rocket explains to Jane Foster why he needs to obtain the Aether. Though funny, it was cut for length.
- A scene between Thor and Jane Foster was also scripted, though not used as the writers figured it had to be Frigga who helps him, and that having Thor converse with Jane and his mother would add to the film's lengthy runtime.
- At one point the filmmakers considered having a confrontation between Thor and his 2013 self in Asgard.
- It was written during Bruce's conversation with the Ancient One that Dormammu would have made a cameo of sorts. When the Ancient One removes the Time Stone from her magical projection, audiences would

have been shown what happens in the split timeline, with Dormammu appearing over Hong Kong.
- After Bruce uses the Nano Gauntlet, he has a conversation with the Hulk at the way station (the pinkish orange landscape where Thanos encountered a young Gamora after using the Infinity Gauntlet in *Avengers: Infinity War*). The scene was written but not filmed.
- In a version of the script, after the Hulk uses the Nano Gauntlet to bring everyone back into existence, all the heroes are reunited at the Avengers compound and the scene then cuts to all eating pizza.
- In a draft of the script, having travelled to the present of the main timeline, the Thanos from the past would have arrived with the head of a decapitated Captain America, tossing it at the feet of present-day Cap. The thinking was that Thanos—waiting for Nebula to transport him to the present of the main timeline—would have travelled to the future in his own timeline and killed the Avengers.
- Nebula from the past wielding the Infinity Gauntlet (as she does in the comics) was scripted. She would have tried to use it in an attempt to prove herself to Thanos and died as a result. It was removed as it undermined Tony's use of it.
- During an IMDb video released to promote *WandaVision* (2021), Paul Bettany revealed to Elizabeth Olsen that a tag scene was considered in which Wanda Maximoff would have opened a body bag drawer revealing the remains of Vision inside. Kevin Feige decided to not have the scene filmed, presumably to avoid spoiling *WandaVision*.
- Shots of Natasha training (firing a gun at a target and hitting a punching bag) and one where she's sitting in the rain were removed. These can be seen in the film's trailers.
- Tony and Pepper are in their cabin preparing lunch. Tony asks if the goji berries are the ones they grew. Pepper replies that they aren't as their alpaca ate them all and has him fetch their daughter for lunch.
- The Hulk attends to the scene of a building fire, rescuing people stuck on the fortieth floor, carrying them down to safety in a satellite dish. He tells the fire chief (played by Reginald VelJohnson) to extinguish the flames using halon bombs before taking a call from Steve Rogers. The scene demonstrates what the Hulk had been up to in the years after the Snap but was removed as the same information was being conveyed in the diner scene. Despite containing unfinished visual effects, it was shown

as part of the bonus footage included with the cinematic re-release of *Endgame*.
- Rhodey and Steve converse in the Avengers meeting room. Steve informs Rhodey that he had to crash the plane he was in during WWII as there were bombs on board, to which Rhodey asks why Steve didn't just jump out of the plane before he crashed it.
- Discussing the Battle of New York, Rocket asks the Avengers how long it took them to defeat the Chitauri. Upon hearing it was several hours, Rocket laughs, noting that the Chitauri are "the suckiest army in the galaxy." In response, Tony shaves off some of Rocket's fur, which makes everyone else laugh.
- Tony checks in on the preparation of the time suit with the Hulk saying someone needs to test it. During test screenings, it was found audiences were still used to the rules of time travel as presented in the *Back to the Future* series and so the scene was rewritten to reinforce the rules *Endgame* was using.
- An alternate version of the Hulk arriving on the roof of the Sanctum Sanctorum has him find the Ancient One relaxing in a chair with a drink. She reveals that Stephen Strange wouldn't be able to help him, as he's yet to learn of the Time Stone.
- On their way to Vormir, Clint and Natasha have a conversation on board the *Benatar*. The scene was initially included to remind audiences of the characters' close relationship, but the filmmakers found it wasn't required.
- The Hulk asks the Ancient One why she didn't deal with Thanos if she knew he had the propensity to misbehave. She then asks him would he have liked it if she interfered with his gamma experiments, to which he replies, "no." Upon hearing this, she gives him the Time Stone and proceeds to explain the rules of time travel. This version wasn't used as the directors felt there wasn't enough conflict in the scene and that the explanation to the rules of time travel needed to be simplified.
- Rocket and Thor arrive in Asgard in 2013. Rocket tries to get an uninterested Thor to focus and complete the mission but it isn't working. Getting the Aether retrieval device from Thor, Rocket asks him for directions, of which Thor is unsure.
- Walking out of the bunker at Camp Lehigh, Howard Stark asks Tony if he would like to work for him, to which Tony replies, "I'm a little tied up in futures right now."

- As Black Widow and Hawkeye decide who will sacrifice themselves to obtain the Soul Stone, Thanos and his forces attack. Hawkeye finds he has to fend off the enemies while trying to stop Black Widow from sacrificing herself and is unable to do so. The filmmakers felt having the enemies in the scene detracted from the moment between Black Widow and Hawkeye and so was rewritten and reshot to add more tension as to who would sacrifice themselves.
- An aerial battle that Kraglin was a part of was cut from the final fight.
- In the middle of the battle with Thanos and his forces, the heroes all meet up in a trench and discuss how to get the Stones to the quantum tunnel in the X-Con Security Consultants van. The scene felt contrived and disrupted the pace of the battle and so was redone.
- As Ant-Man tries to hot wire the X-Con Security Consultants van, he accidentally turns on the radio, which plays the theme to *The Partridge Family* (1970-74), "C'mon Get Happy," attracting the Outriders towards them.
- Having used the Infinity Stones to make Thanos and his army disappear, Tony finds himself at the way station. There he meets an older version of his daughter, Morgan (played by Katherine Langford). She tells him that what he did worked and meant she could grow up but can't reveal what happens to him. Tony, knowing, fears he's made a mistake. Morgan then tells him she's proud of what he did and that she loves him. The scene disrupted the pace of the film, and essentially repeats what Tony says in his own eulogy. Additionally, it was felt audiences had no emotional connection to the older Morgan Stark as she hadn't appeared previously and so was excised.
- With Tony having passed away, Hawkeye gets down on one knee, prompting the other heroes to do the same. The scene was deleted as it was felt it would clash with the subsequent funeral scene, which features a large cast of the Marvel characters.
- Thor has crowned Valkyrie as the new ruler of Asgard. As he departs, she wishes him luck and puts her hand on his shoulder. Thor mistakes this as a sign that she wants to kiss. He leans in but Valkyie asks what he is doing.
- In the *Endgame* trailers, shots of Tony on board the *Benatar* have him appear less gaunt than he does in the final film. Lola Visual Effects had created different iterations of Tony's emaciated look, with the version used in the trailer chosen so as to not reveal the extent of Tony's injuries

until the film's release. Additionally, several scenes used in the trailers were altered so as to not spoil certain scenes: Natasha having a full head of blonde hair when Scott Lang arrives at the Avengers facility (in the film she has red hair with blonde tips); Hulk and Thor being omitted from the group shot when the Avengers finalise which time periods they're going to go back to; Hulk being removed from the shot of Rocket entering Thor's New Asgard residence; Captain America wearing his *Infinity War* outfit (as opposed to his 2012 uniform) when Tony asks Steve, "You trust me?" (this is followed by a handshake that's taken from earlier in the film, with elements altered to make it appear as if it's taking place in the same scene); Captain America strapping a non-broken shield to his arm; the shot of Rocket and War Machine entering the final battle lacking Giant-Man in the background (Rhodey's armour also lacks the red and blue tones); and Captain Marvel sporting her mohawk look as she flies around.

Location, Location

This time around a property off Christopher Road in Sharpsburg, Georgia, fills in for the **Barton family home**. The American headquarters of SANY (318 Cooper Circle, Peachtree City, Georgia)—a heavy equipment manufacturer—stood in for the **Avengers facility** exterior and area where the quantum tunnel is built. The headquarters' interiors were filmed at the now-closed Sheraton Atlanta Airport Hotel, which was located at 1900 Sullivan Road, Atlanta, Georgia. Aerial footage of **Liberty Island** and **Citi Field** (41 Seaver Way, Flushing, New York) were digitally altered to show the effect of people having disappeared.

For the **U-Store-It facility**, the filmmakers returned to a location previously used in *Black Panther*—the Metropolitan Business and Arts District (675 Metropolitan Parkway SW) in Atlanta. Having exited the Quantum Realm, Scott Lang walks down an **empty street**, with the filmmakers using Atlanta's Curran Street NW. The **San Francisco Vanished Memorial** was filmed at Atlanta's Piedmont Park, specifically an area known as the Meadow. The residence at 840 Clemont Drive NE, Atlanta, is once again used as **Cassie's house**.

The cabin situated by Big Lake located on Bouckaert Farm (9445 Browns Lake Road, Fairburn, Georgia) in Chattahoochee Hill country was used as **Tony Stark's cabin**. Fans can actually stay at the location with the three-bedroom guest cabin listed on Airbnb. Steve, Natasha, and Scott meet Bruce Banner at a **diner**. Filming took place at the Landmark Diner Jr located at 2277 Cheshire Bridge Road NE, Atlanta. Those who have seen *Parks and Recreation* (2009-20) may also recognise it as the exterior of JJ's Diner.

Liberty Island

While the film has **New Asgard** (a renamed Tønsberg) in Norway, once again they have a Scottish locale filling the role. This time the fishing village of St Abbs, situated roughly forty-two miles east of Edinburgh, was used. For the **Tokyo street**, however, the filmmakers didn't travel as far, dressing up Broad Street SW (between MLK Jr Drive SW and Mitchell Street SW) in Atlanta. Going back to 2012, the **Manhattan Street** Tony, Steve, Bruce, and Scott land on is actually William Street NW, close to where it intersects with Cone Street NW in Atlanta. Built in the Norman style, Durham Cathedral in Durham, England, was used as the **Asgardian Palace**. For the **lobby of Stark Tower**, the Proscenium (1170 Peachtree Street NE, Atlanta) was used. The exterior of **Camp Lehigh Army Base** was filmed at the Trees Atlanta Operations Center located at 1050 Murphy Avenue, Atlanta. *Endgame* finishes with Steve finally reunited with Peggy, with the house at 1340 Metropolitan Avenue SE, Atlanta, used as **Peggy's home**.

SPIDER-MAN: FAR FROM HOME

Director: Jon Watts
Screenplay: Chris McKenna & Erik Sommers

Producers: Kevin Feige and Amy Pascal
Executive Producers: Louis D'Esposito, Victoria Alonso, Thomas M Hammel, Eric Hauserman Carroll, Rachel O'Connor, Stan Lee, Avi Arad, and Matt Tolmach
Associate Producer: Chris Buongiorno

Cinematography: Matthew J Lloyd
Production Design: Claude Paré
Editing: Dan Lebental and Leigh Folsom Boyd
Music: Michael Giacchino
Costume Design: Anna B Sheppard
Visual Effects Supervisor: Janek Sirrs
Casting: Sarah Halley Finn

Production Companies: Pascal Pictures, Marvel Studios, and Columbia Pictures
Distribution Company: Sony Pictures Releasing

US Release Date: 2 July 2019
Running Time: 129 minutes
Budget: $160 million
Box Office: $1,131,927,996

Based on the Marvel Comics by Stan Lee and Steve Ditko

Cast: Tom Holland (*Peter Parker/Spider-Man*), Samuel L Jackson (*Nick Fury*), Jake Gyllenhaal (*Quentin Beck/Mysterio*), Marisa Tomei (*May Parker*), Jon Favreau (*Happy Hogan*), Zendaya (*MJ*), Jacob Batalon (*Ned Leeds*), Tony Revolori (*Flash Thompson*), Angourie Rice (*Betty Brant*), Remy Hii (*Brad Davis*), Martin Starr (*Mr Harrington*), JB Smoove (*Mr Dell*), Jorge Lendeborg Jr (*Jason Ionello*), Cobie Smulders (*Maria Hill*), Numan Acar (*Dimitri*), Zach Barack (*Zach*), Zoha Rahman (*Zoha*), Yasmin Mwanza (*Yasmin*), Joshua Sinclair-Evans (*Josh*), Tyler Luke Cunningham (*Tyler*), Sebastian Viveros (*Sebastian*), Toni Garrn (*The Seamstress*), Peter Billingsley (*William Ginter Riva*), Clare Dunne (*Victoria*), Nicholas Gleaves (*Guterman*), Claire Rushbrook (*Janice*), J K Simmons (*J Jonah Jameson*), Dawn Michelle King (*E.D.I.T.H.*), Pat Kiernan (*Himself*), Ben Mendelsohn (*Talos*), Sharon Blynn (*Soren*)

While on a school trip to Europe, Peter Parker is tasked by Nick Fury to help in combating elemental creatures from another dimension.

Despite *Avengers: Endgame* being an ending to The Infinity Saga, many questions from the fallout remain unanswered. While some of it was to set up the upcoming Phase Four, some threads would be explored in *Spider-Man: Far From Home*, the film acting as an epilogue to The Infinity Saga.

Sony Pictures Entertainment announced plans for a follow up film to *Spider-Man: Homecoming* in early December 2016, before the first film was even released, and setting a release date of 5 July 2019. Jon Watts would return as director along with writers Chris McKenna and Erik Sommers. It was revealed that the *Spider-Man* sequel would take place not too long after *Endgame* and explore some of the ramifications of people returning from the Snap five years later as well as how Peter Parker copes with the death of his mentor, Tony Stark.

The main cast from the previous film return including Tom Holland, Zendaya, Jon Favreau, Jacob Batalon, Martin Starr, and Marisa Tomei. Established MCU actors making an appearance in Spidey's film this time around are Samuel L Jackson as Nick Fury and Cobie Smulders as Maria Hill.

Jake Gyllenhaal was cast as Quentin Beck/Mysterio—a member of Spider-Man's rogues' gallery yet to be adapted into a live-action film. While comic book fans correctly surmised the character would be the villain of the movie, Mysterio's allegiance was kept ambiguous during *Far From Home*'s marketing so as to preserve the film's twist for audiences at large. This isn't the first time the actor has been linked to a Spidey film, with Gyllenhaal considered as a replacement for Tobey Maguire when the Spider-Man actor injured his back prior to work on 2004's *Spider-Man 2*. (Some sources reported this was a tactic Sony attempted to prevent Maguire from leaving the project due to pay disputes—one that worked.)

On 23 June 2018, Tom Holland revealed the film's title—*Spider-Man: Far From Home*—via an Instagram video. Principal photography began the following month, with the production based in Leavesden, England. This was particularly beneficial for Holland who lives in London. Production then relocated to Prague and Liberec in the Czech Republic, followed by Venice and finally New York City. Filming wrapped on 16 October 2018.

Far From Home has a contemporary relevance with its theme of fake news, with many instances of misdirection being a key feature of the plot. Following on from the revelation that Quentin Beck isn't actually a hero but a disgruntled former Stark Industries employee, he and Spider-Man engage in an illusion battle. Framestore were tasked with creating the visual effects for the mostly digital sequence. The studio worked with Watts and visual effects supervisor Janek Sirrs in coming up with the various nightmarish scenarios Mysterio puts Spider-Man in. The comic books, the animated short *Duck Amuck* (1953), the fight scene with multiple Agent Smiths from *The Matrix Reloaded* (2003), and the title sequence to *Spectre* (2015) all served as inspiration. Concept art was created and the ideas storyboarded. Holland's movements were captured using motion capture and used where possible. Throughout the different illusions, digital green smoke is ever present, adding a sense of unease (for example, in the school hallway dry ice-esque smoke blankets the ground). After Spider-Man is shown Tony Stark's gravestone, a zombie Iron Man pops up from the ground and chases him. The design of the zombie Iron Man had to be scary but not appear too gruesome according to Framestore. Different ideas were tried, including one where the character had decaying flesh and another in which he was more skeletal. For the Iron Man armour itself, the look of broken Ultron Sentries with their wires and metal pieces sticking out from *Avengers: Age of Ultron* (2015) was used as reference. All up, the sequence took nine months to complete.

One of the film's biggest surprises would be the public revealing of Spider-Man's secret identity. Bigger still is the introduction of J Jonah Jameson into the MCU, played by none other than J K Simmons. Simmons previously played the publisher of the *Daily Bugle* in Sam Raimi's *Spider-Man* trilogy, making him the first actor to play the same Marvel character in two different Marvel film universes. Simmons was approached about the role as late as possible to keep his potential involvement a surprise—a risky move given the filmmakers weren't sure how he would respond. After calling Raimi and getting his blessing, Simmons signed on. His cameo was filmed in front of a green screen set up in a conference room at the Marvel offices. With the *Daily Bugle* reimagined as a news website, a fictional website was later created to promote the film's home media release.

On 26 June 2019, *Spider-Man: Far From Home* had its world premiere at Grauman's Chinese Theatre in Hollywood. *Far From Home* would go on to gross over $1.1 billion worldwide, becoming the first Spider-Man film to gross over $1 billion worldwide, and making it Sony Pictures' highest grossing film (surpassing the 2012 James Bond film *Skyfall*). Many critics reviewed the film favourably, with praise for the cast, while audiences found *Spider-Man: Far From Home* to be a thrilling adventure filled with plenty of heart and humour. Although The Infinity Saga was now complete, it wouldn't be the end of the Marvel Cinematic Universe.

Mid-Credits Scene
Spider-Man places MJ down near Madison Square Garden. He proceeds to watch a breaking news cast on a jumbotron. Footage of Quentin Beck is shown in which he reveals that Spider-Man's real identity is Peter Parker.

Post-Credits Scene
Soren reveals that she's been disguised as Maria Hill, with her husband, Talos, pretending to be Nick Fury. Talos reports to the real Fury who, it turns out, has been taking some time off on a space station.

Marvellous Miscellanea
- Cinematographer Matthew J Lloyd reunites with Watts, the pair having previously worked together on *Cop Car* (2015).
- *Far From Home*'s initial working title was reportedly *Fall of George*. It later used the name *Bosco*—another *Seinfeld* (1989-98) reference—the word being George Costanza's ATM code.
- The use of the colour red was kept to a minimum in the set design to ensure the Spider-Man suit would stand out more.
- J B Smoove was added to the cast as Mr Dell, after the filmmakers saw

an Audi commercial featuring the actor. The ad in question was created as a tie-in with *Spider-Man: Homecoming* and saw Smoove's character conducting Peter Parker's driving test.
- In Venice, the students stay at Hotel DeMatteis, a nod to J M DeMatteis who has written many Spider-Man comics. Additional shout-outs to Spidey writers come in the form of signs that can be seen in the city: Calle Bendiso (Brian Michael Bendis), Calle Slotto (Dan Slott), Calle Sterno (Roger Stern), Calle Michelinio (David Michelinie), and Calle G Convayo (Gerry Conway).
- When Peter is looking at MJ posing with pigeons in Venice, look closely and you can actually spot Quentin Beck wearing a blue shirt and cap in the background behind Peter. Additionally, when Peter is walking with MJ after he buys the black dahlia, they pass Gutes Guterman.
- Objects in the bar scene were included to subliminally influence Peter to give Quentin the glasses. Military medals are there to remind Peter to be a hero, an image of glasses helps keep the item top of mind, a left turn arrow could connote the need for a change in direction, and the song that's playing is "Town Called Malice" by The Jam which has the theme of being unhappy with one's situation but having the ability to change things.
- Gutes Guterman is named after Dan Guterman, a writer who's worked on *Community* (2009-15) and *Rick and Morty* (2013-).
- During Spider-Man's swing through New York City, he takes a selfie whilst doing the peace sign. The pose is reminiscent to the one players can do while taking selfies in Insomniac's 2018 *Spider-Man* video game.
- At the end of the film when Spidey meets up with MJ, a sign behind them says, "We are so excited to show you what comes next!" Under this is a '1', '2', and '3', with a '?' at the end. This refers to the first three phases of the MCU and the then-forthcoming Phase Four.
- Tom Holland took home a pair of Tony Stark's glasses used in the film. In fact, the actor has admitted to taking a prop from every project he's worked on.
- With the first trailer being released before *Endgame* hit theatres, early marketing material for *Far From Home* intentionally didn't include any references to his disappearance or how he comes back to life. Exactly when the film is set in relation to the third and fourth *Avengers* films is downplayed, the teaser trailer going so far as to feature Spider-Man

wearing his classic red and blue suit when he appears at the homeless support charity dinner and a shot of Spidey swinging through New York with the former Avengers Tower shown in the middle of its re-design.

From Panels to the Screen

In the comics, Aunt May has worked for F.E.A.S.T. (Food, Emergency Aid, Shelter, and Training), an organization that helps the homeless. This is alluded to in the film, with her cinematic counterpart working for the Salvation Army. A poster featuring Crusher Hogan and advertising a one-hundred-dollar prize can be seen in the kitchen of the Urban Sports and Cultural Center. Crusher Hogan is the wrestler Peter Parker beats in *Amazing Fantasy* #15 (1962), with one hundred dollars being the amount he earns for doing so. And while partially obscured, another name that's listed could be Bone Saw McGraw, the wrestler Peter fights in the 2002 film *Spider-Man*. The suitcase Peter uses bears the initials BFP, referring to Benjamin Parker, Peter's uncle in the source material (his middle name has yet to be canonically revealed).

Ned Leeds and Betty Brant become a couple in the film. In the comics, Ned and Betty also dated each other before marrying in *The Amazing Spider-Man* #156 (1976). Two new characters at Peter's school are derived from the comics. The first is Mr Del. In both media, Mr Del (spelt "Dell" in the film) is a teacher at Peter's school (he's specifically a science teacher in the comic books). The second character is Brad Davis. The cinematic version of Brad Davis competes with Peter for MJ's attention. He bears a similarity to his comic book counterpart who's a quarterback at Empire State University and has been on a date with MJ.

Far From Home sees Mysterio pretending to be a hero and tricking the public into believing Spider-Man is a criminal, which is essentially the story told in his debut issue—*The Amazing Spider-Man* #13 (1964). In the comics, Quentin Beck/Mysterio was a movie special effects artist and stuntman who sought a quick path to fame by trying to frame and kill Spider-Man. Though he doesn't possess any powers, Quentin's costume contains various weaponry he can employ in combat. Parts of his suit can emit a smokescreen and hallucinogenic gas, which he often uses in tandem with his hologram projectors to disorient his foes. The crystal ball-esque helmet he dons—that he can see out of, but others can't see into—contains a sonar device that allows him to "see" through the smoke around him. His gloves can dispel a web-dissolving acid while his cape would electrically shock anyone who touched it.

In the film, Quentin Beck says he's from Earth 833, while Peter's reality is Earth Dimension 616. This follows the multiverse naming convention used in the comics. The mainstream Marvel Universe is known as Earth-616, Earth-833 is where Billy Braddock/Spider-UK comes from, while the world of the 2018 *Spider-Man* video game has been designated Earth-1048. For those curious, Sam Raimi's *Spider-Man* trilogy takes place on Earth-96283, while Marc Webb's two Spidey films are set on Earth-120703.

Though not a direct adaption of anything from the source material, the stealth suit Nick Fury gives Peter in the movie was inspired by two costumes from the comics: the black costume worn by Spider-Man Noir of Earth-90214 and the stealth costume (which has a camouflage mode) Peter develops early on in the "Big Time" story arc (*The Amazing Spider-Man* #648-656, 2010-11).

In the comics, the Elementals are a group of beings that hail from another universe, each of whom can control one of the elements. Hellfire has mastery over flames, Hydron can command water, Magnum is able to manipulate earth, and Zephyr has power over air. For the film, however, director Jon Watts decided to amalgamate the concept of the Elementals with some of Spidey's classic foes.

The MCU Earth Elemental takes some inspiration from Sandman. Flint Marko, having escaped from prison, hides on a beach where nuclear tests are conducted. After a nuclear explosion, he finds his body has taken on the properties of sand. The Water Elemental is based on Hydro-Man. During a battle between Spider-Man and Namor on board the USS *Bulldog*, crewman Morris "Morrie" Bench was knocked overboard, falling into the water just as an experimental generator was being tested. The energy from the device combined with underwater volcanic gases granted him the ability to turn his body into water. In the film, Hydro-Man's origin story from the comics is cited by Flash as a possible explanation for the existence of the Water Elemental. The Fire Elemental resembles Molten Man. Mark Raxton's skin turned to metal after he's covered with a liquid metal alloy that was created from substances found inside a meteor. He finds that he now has super strength, possesses skin that is highly resistant to injury, and is also able to generate intense heat, giving his body a molten form. The Air Elemental, meanwhile, could be based on Cyclone. Andre Gerard was an engineer who invented a weapon known as the Cyclone. With NATO not wanting to use his creation, he instead incorporated the technology into a suit that could create high-speed winds around him.

Despite the film not featuring direct adaptations of Sandman, Hydro-Man, Molten Man, and Cyclone, the debut issues of each character are referenced in *Far From Home*. When Fury and Maria Hill are shooting the Earth Elemental, '462' can be seen as part of a car's number plate (*The Amazing Spider-Man* #4, 1963; Sandman's first appearance), Fury's car in Prague bears the number plate "ASM 28965" (*The Amazing Spider-Man* #28, 1965, which was published in September; Molten Man's first appearance), an overturned car on Tower Bridge has "TASM 143" as its plate (*The Amazing Spider-Man* #143, 1975; Cyclone's first appearance), and though not in the final cut of the film—but present in the trailers—"Asm 212" can be seen on a boat in Venice (*The Amazing Spider-Man* #212, 1981; Hydro-Man's first appearance).

Speaking of number plates, the one on the car Fury drives in Berlin is "MTU 83779," a reference to *Marvel Team-Up* #83 published in July 1979. The issue sees Spider-Man and Nick Fury team up against Silver Samurai and Boomerang. In addition to being Cyclone's debut issue, *The Amazing Spider-Man* #143 is also the issue in which Peter and MJ first kiss, hence the "TASM 143" number plate appearing on-screen when Peter and MJ kiss in the film. And lastly, in the post-credits scene (which revealed that Talos has been masquerading as Nick Fury) we see the number plate of Talos' car, "HNM 62011." This is a reference to *Hawkeye & Mockingbird* #6 (2011) in which a Skrull impersonating Nick Fury is discovered.

This cinematic incarnation of MJ reveals to Peter that she knows he's Spider-Man, with her comic book counterpart doing the same in *The Amazing Spider-Man* #257 (1984). Spider-Man contending with a giant Mysterio and seeing his reflection in a series of mirrors are events that occur in *The Amazing Spider-Man* #67 (1968). While the zombie Iron Man we see in the film was merely an illusion, there actually is a zombie Iron Man in the comics. That version of the character hails from Earth-2149 where all the Marvel heroes have been turned into zombies.

Among the various hologram Spider-Man suit options are designs that hark back to the comics. One bears a resemblance to the Superior Spider-Man suit (has a large spider chest emblem that spans shoulder to shoulder), while another looks like the Iron Spider suit (identifiable by the four mechanical arms). Soon after, one that appears to be based on the Spider Armor Mk II is shown (has a large spider chest emblem that stretches from the bottom of the neck down to the groin).

Though it is a newspaper in the mainstream comic continuity, the *Daily*

Bugle is a news website in the film. Both iterations, though, have an anti-Spider-Man slant. In the Ultimate Universe, however, the publication did eventually go digital-only, doing so in *Ultimate Comics Spider-Man* #11 (2010). The website in the issue is dailybugle.com; in the film it's thedailybugle.net.

The comic book version of J Jonah Jameson is known for being the executive editor, publisher, and owner of the *Daily Bugle*. His MCU counterpart is bald whereas his Earth-616 and Earth-96283 incarnations have a full head of hair (Simmons wore a wig to portray the character in Raimi's *Spider-Man* trilogy). Spider-Man's identity has been revealed in the comics—accidentally or otherwise—to members of the public several times. Mysterio does this in the MCU, but in *Civil War* #2 (2006) Peter does so himself in a news conference as a way of showing his support for the Superhuman Registration Act.

MCU Easter Eggs

Tony Stark's death, which occurred at the end of *Avengers: Endgame*, is a big part of the film. Pictures of Tony, along with Captain America, Black Widow, and Vision, can be seen as part of the in memoriam video created by students at Midtown School of Science & Technology. The effects of Thanos using the Infinity Gauntlet are explored, referring to the subsequent return of those that disappeared as the Blip.

Happy Hogan hands May a large cheque to support the homeless, signed by Pepper Potts. Videos about the Snap, Wakanda (*Finding Wakanda*), Hydra (*Hunting Hydra*), Einstein Rosen Bridges (featuring Erik Selvig), and Iron Man (*Heart of Iron: The Tony Stark Story*) can be seen as part of the in-flight entertainment during Peter's flight to Venice. Other heroes are named-dropped: Thor (who's off-world), Doctor Strange (who's unavailable to help Fury), and Captain Marvel (Fury tells Peter not to invoke her name).

We find out that Quentin Beck was the one who invented B.A.R.F. and was present backstage during Tony's demonstration of it at MIT in *Captain America: Civil War*. William Ginter Riva—who we first met in *Iron Man* (2008)—has joined Quentin in his revenge against Tony. Before Maria Hill alerts Fury to an electromagnetic pulse in London, Fury mentions the presence of Kree sleeper cells and that this information was top secret. Spider-Man glides through the hole of the building formerly known as Avengers Tower on his way to meet MJ. And in the post-credits scene, we find out that Talos and his wife, Soren, have been impersonating Fury and Maria Hill respectively, throughout the course of the film.

Chopped, Changed, and Lengthened

- It was written at one point that Spider-Man would publicly reveal his secret identity during the final battle. Writers Chris McKenna and Erik Sommers even tried having Mysterio dupe Spider-Man into doing so. Neither was used as the writers felt it undermined Spider-Man's victory.
- During a recording of *Midtown News*, Betty Brant and Jason Ionello vanish as a result of Thanos using the Infinity Gauntlet. Cutting to a new shot, we see them blip back, surprising the new reporter who has replaced them.
- Peter carries out several errands before his trip, including the purchases of a travel adaptor and dual headphone adaptor from Delmar's Deli-Grocery, selling his toys, picking up his passport, and taking down the Manfredi mob as Spider-Man. The sequence—dubbed *Peter's To-Do List*—was cut to increase the film's pace. It was included with the *Far From Home* theatrical re-release and was marketed as a short film included with the film's home media release.
- Various clips of the students and teachers going through border security in Italy were filmed. This includes Flash, who indicates to the border security guard that he's not with the rest of the school group, and Peter, who begins to explain he's on a school trip but is quickly given his passport back to proceed with his travels.
- Many moments involving Mr Dell and Mr Harrington were filmed. These include: Mr Dell asking Mr Harrington how he booked the Venice hotel, to which he replies he used the Italian version of Yelp; Mr Dell giving an explanation to his students on a building in Venice; Mr Dell warning the students that the waters of Venice contain a bacteria that can cause leptospirosis; Mr Harrington searching his pockets for a reference sheet in the Prague hotel lobby, only to recall that it's on the bus; and Mr Harrington at Newark Liberty International Airport remarking that he got everyone back home safe.
- On their way to Prague, the group stop at a small town for a quick break. While Peter meets with an associate of Nick Fury's, Mr Dell tries to find the bathroom, Mr Harrington tries to work out where they are, and the other students explore the deli.
- Various clips of Flash's live streams to his followers were filmed. These include when he's in the deli, when he's on the bus in London, and Flash running from the Elemental attack in London.

- The scene in which Tony Stark drunkenly destroys objects with his repulsors at his party from *Iron Man 2* (2010) was edited to include Guterman in it. He would have gotten a shard of glass in his eye, prompting his hatred of Tony Stark. It was felt that there wasn't a need to show that all of Quentin's crew had previously worked for Tony and so was cut.
- Quentin Beck and his crew are in a parking garage. He tells Victoria to activate the EMP generator after which Quentin receives a call from Fury, asking Quentin to go to London. The scene was edited back into the film for *Far From Home*'s theatrical re-release.
- Martin Starr has revealed that he filmed a scene in which Mr Harrington and the students run along the River Thames and stop to witness Mysterio fighting the Elemental. He tells the students to keep running while he asks the Elemental to attack him instead.
- On the plane home from London, Peter sleeps on MJ's shoulder. They wake up, look at each other, and go back to sleep.
- An extended version of May picking Peter up from the airport sees him asking her how he looks with Tony's glasses on.
- To avoid *Endgame* spoilers, the teaser trailer depicts Spidey wearing his classic red and blue outfit at the homeless support charity dinner instead of the Iron Spider suit. Additionally, in the official trailer, Nick Fury says, "Beck is from Earth; just not ours," whereas in the final film he says, "Mr Beck is from Earth; just not yours," thus preserving the twist that Talos has taken Fury's place. Other bits of footage not used in the final film include the Italian customs officer holding up Peter's Spider-Man suit (Peter says they're his pyjamas), Peter replying with, "No banana. Great," after the Italian customs officer tells him he can't bring the fruit into the country having found it in his suitcase, Betty taking a picture of Ned during their boat ride into Venice, Peter asking Fury if Ned will be fine (Fury having tranquilized Ned) and Fury responding that Peter might want to turn him over so he doesn't swallow his tongue, and the various Spider-Man suit holograms being coloured instead of blue and white.

Location, Location

The film opens with Nick Fury and Maria Hill encountering the Earth Elemental in **Ixtenco, Mexico**. The ruined village of Belchite in Spain stands in for the Mexican location. Situated about forty kilometres south east of Zaragoza, the village was destroyed during the Spanish Civil War and currently serves as a war memorial. The homeless support charity dinner was held at the **Urban Sports and Cultural Center**, which is located at 5 Stuyvesant Avenue in Brooklyn, New York. Interiors of the venue were filmed at the York Hall Leisure Centre (5 Old Ford Road) in London, England.

Beginning their field trip in Italy, Peter Parker and his friends fly into **Venice Marco Polo Airport** (Viale Galileo Galilei, 30/1, 30173 Tessera-Venezia), which is actually located on the mainland. The group then head into the historic centre of Venice, travelling down the **Grand Canal** by boat, and going underneath the **Rialto Bridge** (the bridge and surrounding area were also recreated as a set at Warner Bros. Studios Leavesden located on Warner Drive in Leavesden, England). After checking in to the **Hotel DeMatteis** (the fictional accommodation can be found on Fondamenta Sant'Anna, close to Calle Crosera), the group then visits Piazza San Marco, known in English as **St Mark's Square**. Mr Harrington tries to take a selfie along the **Riva degli Schiavoni**. Peter heads to an **antique shop** at the northern end of Corte Semenzi. As Mysterio leads the Water Elemental away from the canal, we see people running across the **Ponte dei Conzafelzi**. While it appears Mr Harrington and some of the students are going to the **Leonardo da Vinci Museum**, they are in fact standing outside the western façade of the Santa Maria Formosa (Fondamenta Santa Maria Formosa, Castello 5263, 30122 Venezia). The Leonardo da Vinci Museum is real though and can be found at Campo San Rocco, San Polo 3052, 30125 Venezia. The fight against the Water Elemental culminates in **Campo Santa Maria Formosa**. Nick Fury takes Peter on a trip down the **Canal de le Galeazze**—behind them you can see the Venetian Arsenal. The **command centre** they arrive at, however, was a set built in the UK. Preparing to head off to their next destination, the group walks down **Calle del Slotto**—in actuality it's Calle del Vento—and onto **Campo de R Sterno** (which is actually Campo de S Basegio). The bus was parked between the Terminal San Basilio and Ponte Molin.

The bus drives down **Strada Regionale 48 delle Dolomiti** in northeastern Italy, passing through a tunnel that was carved from the mountain itself. Peter calls a drone to take Brad out as the bus drives down the **Strada Provinciale 24 del Passo Valparola** in Italy (you see them pass the Rifugio Passo Valparola bar and restaurant). When we see the group arrive in Prague, capital of the Czech Republic, the bus is travelling north on **Na Kampě**, driving underneath Charles Bridge (or *Karlův most* in Czech). The hotel the group stays at in

Charles Bridge *Tower Bridge*

Prague is the **Carlo IV** (Senovážné náměstí 13/991, 110 00 Praha 1). The hotel's upper floor, however, was actually shot at a country club in London. The **Czech castle** where Peter, Nick Fury, and Mysterio have a meeting is actually Hatfield House in Hatfield, England. **Peter jumps down onto some steps**, startling an elderly couple on Radnické schody (close to where it intersects with Loretánská). Further down Radnické schody is where we see **Mr Harrington lead the group to see an opera**. The opera is being performed at the **Vinohrady Theatre** (or *Divadlo na Vinohradech* in Czech) located at náměstí Míru 7, 120 00 Praha 2. For the **carnival** where the fight with the Fire Elemental takes place, the filmmakers dressed up Dr Edvard Beneš Sqaure in Liberec, a city northeast of Prague. It's on **Charles Bridge** that Peter confesses to MJ that he's Spider-Man. Previous films to have featured the landmark include *Mission: Impossible* (1996), *XXX* (2002), and *Van Helsing* (2004).

The Alexandra Palace Theatre (Alexandra Palace Way, London) was used as the **abandoned theatre** where Quentin Beck and his crew plan their next attack. Spider-Man travels to Berlin by hitching a ride on a train, doing so from **Prague Main Railway Station** (or *Praha hlavní nádraží* in Czech). While the film has us believe he has arrived in Berlin, **Peter meeting up with Nick Fury** was filmed outside London's West Silvertown DLR Station. Scenes set at the **German Europol offices** were filmed at Holland Park School (Airlie Gardens, Campden Hill Road) in London. However, the office is an illusion, with Quentin Beck disguising a **derelict building**. For this, the filmmakers used Millennium Mills, a former flour mill located in the Royal Docks area of London. Peter finds himself at **Broek op Langedijk's town square** which was created in the courtyard of a Prague restaurant, while the **tulip field** where Happy lands was shot in London (the airstair was there, but the rest of the jet, tulips, and windmill were all added in via CGI). The scene where

Maria informs Fury about the next Elemental attack in London was filmed at Moretown office campus (Thomas More Street, London).

Arriving in London, Peter's classmates alight at **St Pancras International**. The filmmakers had one morning to shoot at the actual **Tower Bridge** and so recreated the London landmark to be able to shoot much of the action sequence that takes place there. With all the chaos happening on the bridge, Mr Harrington leads the children away to **Tower Wharf**. Fury oversees the battle from **The Shard**. Located at 32 London Bridge Street, London, it is currently the UK's tallest building. Happy meets up with MJ, Ned, Betty, and Flash, and they all subsequently run into the **Tower of London**. Exteriors of the castle were shot on location, with the interiors constructed as a set at Warner Bros. Studios Leavesden. After Peter defeats Mysterio, Happy has a chat with Fury and Maria by the water on **Thames Path** (it can be accessed from St Katherine's Way).

London Stansted Airport, located off the M11 motorway in the English county of Essex, stands in for **Newark Liberty International Airport**. Back home in New York, Spider-Man meets MJ on **Park Avenue** (between E 40th Street and E 41st Street) before taking her for a swing. They land at the **corner of W 33rd Street and Eighth Avenue** (on the same block as the James A Farley Building), before watching a breaking news cast on the **Madison Square Garden** (4 Pennsylvania Plaza, New York) jumbotron. In the post-credits scene, the establishing shot sees "Fury" and "Maria" travelling east on **Gresham Street** (between Foster Lane and Gutter Lane) in London.

EXTENDED CUT

In a similar vein to *Avengers: Endgame*, *Spider-Man: Far From Home* was given a theatrical re-release. The extended edition hit theatres on 29 August 2019—ahead of the United States' Labor Day Weekend—and consisted of four minutes of additional footage including Peter Parker completing chores before his European trip and Quentin Beck talking with his crew before the London attack.

APPENDICES

LIST OF INFINITY STONES

Space Stone
Colour: Blue
Appears in: *Thor* (inside the Tesseract), *Captain America: The First Avenger* (inside the Tesseract), *The Avengers* (inside the Tesseract), *Thor: Ragnarok* (inside the Tesseract), *Avengers: Infinity War*, *Captain Marvel* (inside the Tesseract), *Avengers: Endgame*
Can be used to create portals and its energies can power weaponry. It was housed within the Tesseract.

Mind Stone
Colour: Yellow
Appears in: *The Avengers* (inside Loki's sceptre), *Captain America: The Winter Soldier* (inside Loki's sceptre), *Avengers: Age of Ultron*, *Captain America: Civil War*, *Avengers: Infinity War*, *Avengers: Endgame*
Allows the user to control minds, project energy, and can be used to empower humans. It was initially housed inside a golden sceptre and later embedded into Vision's forehead.

Reality Stone
Colour: Red
Appears in: *Thor: The Dark World*, *Avengers: Infinity War*, *Avengers: Endgame*
Also known as the Aether, it enables the wielder to alter matter. While it has a stone form like the other relics, it can exist as a fluid.

Power Stone
Colour: Purple
Appears in: *Guardians of the Galaxy*, *Avengers: Infinity War*, *Avengers: Endgame*
Grants the wielder enormous destructive power. It was housed inside the Orb.

Time Stone
Colour: Green
Appears in: *Doctor Strange*, *Thor: Ragnarok* (inside the Eye of Agamotto), *Avengers: Infinity War*, *Avengers: Endgame*
Allows the user to manipulate time. It was housed within the Eye of Agamotto.

Soul Stone
Colour: Orange
Appears in: *Avengers: Infinity War*, *Avengers: Endgame*
Allows the user to manipulate the souls of others. To obtain it requires a sacrifice.

THE INFINITY SAGA IN CHRONOLOGICAL ORDER

The following lists the films in The Infinity Saga in a rough chronological order, using the time period each film is predominantly set in to determine its placement. Some films/events overlap with one another and are noted as such. Though Marvel Studios does keep track of the MCU chronology (after being hired to direct *Spider-Man: Homecoming*, Jon Watts was shown a scroll containing a timeline of the MCU), Kevin Feige has revealed that, with a few exceptions, the studio doesn't usually outright state the years in which a film's events take place. Along with contradictions within and between the films themselves, this makes it difficult for viewers to construct a precise timeline of events.

Captain America: The First Avenger
Intertitles reveal Johann Schmidt stole the Tesseract in March 1942. The World Exposition of Tomorrow is held in 1943, with a newspaper indicating Steve Rogers is given the Super-Soldier serum later that same year. World War II's end in 1945 is depicted.

Captain Marvel
A calendar seen at Maria Rambeau's residence indicates *Captain Marvel* largely takes place during 1995.

Iron Man
The screen Pepper Potts watches an episode of *Mad Money* on bears the date 4 May 2008. *Iron Man* taking place in 2008 is further corroborated in *Captain America: Civil War*, which takes place in 2016. In *Civil War*, Vision says Tony Stark announced that he was Iron Man eight years ago.

Iron Man 2
An intertitle indicates *Iron Man 2* takes place six months after *Iron Man*.

The Incredible Hulk
A news report of the Hulk's rampage at Culver University can be seen in *Iron Man 2* when Tony Stark is hired as a consultant for S.H.I.E.L.D., suggesting

the events of both films overlap. In fact, the official timeline from *The Art of Marvel's The Avengers* book reveals Bruce Banner's transformation into the Hulk at a bottling plant in Brazil occurs around the same time as Iron Man's battle against Ivan Vanko in Monaco.

Thor
It's established in *Iron Man 2* that events from that film overlap with *Thor* (Agent Coulson leaves in the middle of *Iron Man 2* to investigate Mjolnir's appearance on Earth). However, this is contradicted in *The Avengers*—which is set in 2012—when Nick Fury says Thor arrived in Puente Antiguo the previous year. Regardless of the year in which *Thor* is set, the film should be watched after *Iron Man 2*, but before *The Avengers*.

The Avengers
An intertitle in *Avengers: Endgame* indicates *The Avengers* takes place in 2012.

Iron Man 3
When Maya Hansen visits Tony at his mansion, he says to her, "Please don't tell me there's a twelve-year-old kid waiting in the car that I've never met." This implies that *Iron Man 3* takes place around Christmas of 2012 (Tony and Maya having slept together on 1 January 2000). However, Maya jokingly corrects him, replying that the child is actually thirteen. This would place the events of the film around Christmas 2013. This is backed up by a newspaper in the film—which reported Tony's presumed death due to the Mandarin's attack on his mansion—bearing the date 23 December 2013. This list assumes 2012 is correct as, in correspondence with the author, *Iron Man 3* co-writer Drew Pearce revealed that he was working with the idea that the film was set about six to eight months after the events of *The Avengers*.

Thor: The Dark World
An intertitle in *Avengers: Endgame* indicates *Thor: The Dark World* takes place in 2013.

Captain America: The Winter Soldier
The date stamp seen in the footage of Georges Batroc's interrogation indicates *Captain America: The Winter Soldier* takes place in 2013. Steve Rogers tells Natasha Romanoff that he's ninety-five years old, which could place the film in

either 2013 or 2014 depending on the month the film is set (in *Captain America: The First Avenger* we found out that Steve was born on 4 July 1918). Prior to the release of *The Winter Soldier*, Scarlett Johansson revealed in an interview that the film is set two years after *The Avengers*. Given the discrepancy, *Captain America: The Winter Soldier* should be seen after *Thor: The Dark World*.

Guardians of the Galaxy

Guardians of the Galaxy takes place in 2014, with most of the film occurring twenty-six years after the opening flashback set in 1988. An intertitle in *Avengers: Endgame* also indicates *Guardians of the Galaxy* takes place in 2014.

Guardians of the Galaxy Vol. 2

Guardians of the Galaxy Vol. 2 is set in 2014, a few months after *Guardians of the Galaxy* (the bulk of the film taking place thirty-four years after the opening flashback which is set in 1980, as indicated by an intertitle).

Avengers: Age of Ultron

Events from *Captain America: The Winter Soldier* are referenced, placing *Avengers: Age of Ultron* after that film.

Ant-Man

The Avengers' fight with Ultron in Sokovia is mentioned in a newspaper and later referenced by Hank Pym, placing *Ant-Man* after *Avengers: Age of Ultron*.

Captain America: Civil War

A newspaper in *Captain America: Civil War* reveals the film takes place in 2016.

Doctor Strange

Stephen Strange's car accident occurs on 2 February 2016. The events in the film take place over roughly a year (although when certain events in the film happen in relation to other MCU entries is unclear). Given the expanse of time *Doctor Strange* covers, it can be seen any time after *Ant-Man* but before *Thor: Ragnarok*.

Black Panther

A BBC news report indicates *Black Panther* is set a week after T'Chaka's death (as seen in *Captain America: Civil War*).

Spider-Man: Homecoming

The film recaps Peter Parker's trip to Germany with the bulk of the film taking place two months after he arrives home. The intertitle that states *Spider-Man: Homecoming* is set eight years after the Battle of New York appears to be incorrect, something which Joe Russo has acknowledged.

Thor: Ragnarok

Thor tells Bruce Banner that the battle against Ultron in Sokovia occurred two years ago (as seen in *Avengers: Age of Ultron*). The mid-credits scene leads into *Avengers: Infinity War*.

Ant-Man and the Wasp

Scott Lang has served the majority of his two-year house arrest by the time *Ant-Man and the Wasp* begins, with Scott telling Jimmy Woo that he has three days remaining (Scott completes his sentence by the end of the film). The mid-credits scene depicts Hank Pym, Janet van Dyne, and Hope van Dyne disappearing due to Thanos using the Infinity Gauntlet, an event that occurs at the end of *Avengers: Infinity War*.

Avengers: Infinity War

Tony tells Doctor Strange that he's been thinking about Thanos for six years (since the Battle of New York in 2012), which means *Avengers: Infinity War* takes place in 2018. The film itself takes place over two days.

Avengers: Endgame

The beginning of *Avengers: Endgame* takes place twenty-two days after *Infinity War* (as heard during Tony's recording to Pepper). The story then jumps forward five years after Thor kills Thanos.

Spider-Man: Far From Home

A *Midtown News* segment reveals *Spider-Man: Far From Home* is set eight months after *Avengers: Endgame*.

ACKNOWLEDGEMENTS

Thank you to my esteemed editors Keelan Judge and Lauren Pearce. Once again, you've both done an incredible job and I can never thank you enough.

As always, thank you to Joey Nguyen, Morris Umali, and Alexander Warton for all their help, guidance, suggestions, and the occasional praise.

Thank you to Melvin Tu for answering my many music-related questions. You're a lifesaver! Thank you to Tina Oh for her translation of Korean websites, which helped in my research for *Black Panther*.

Many thanks to Jason Morris and Scott Sheens for helping me with the From Panels to the Screen sections. Working out where certain scenes are filmed is sometimes tricky, but I was able to complete each section thanks to the help of "Jovial" Jay Shepard. Thank you to Markus Raymond, the main editor of the Appendix to the Handbook of the Marvel Universe, for clarifying a few things about the Marvel Universe for me.

I am extremely grateful to actor and stuntman Shane Rangi for answering my questions about his work on *Thor: Ragnarok*. *Kia ora*!

Special thanks to Matthew Lin for his help with the book design and Kelvin Wong for his support of the book.

And finally, to all those that have contributed to the Marvel Cinematic Universe—from the actors to the runners, and all the other roles that allow a film to be made—thank you for creating one of the best franchises ever.

BIBLIOGRAPHY

The audio commentaries and other special features on the various Marvel Cinematic Universe home media releases were the main sources of information for this book. In addition to the numerous comic book issues referred to throughout the text, the following resources were used.

Books

Bray, Adam. *Marvel Studios Visual Dictionary*. London: Dorling Kindersley Limited, 2018.

Bray, Adam, Lorraine Cink, Melanie Scott, and Stephen Wiacek. *Ultimate Marvel*. London: Dorling Kindersley Limited, 2017.

Brevoort, Tom, Tom DeFalco, Matthew K Manning, and Peter Sanderson. *Marvel Year by Year: A Visual Chronicle*. London: Dorling Kindersley Limited, 2013.

Christiansen, Jeff, Mike Fichera, Stuart Vandal, Mark O'English, Sean McQuaid, Madison Carter, Michael Hoskin, et al. *Official Handbook of the Marvel Universe A to Z Vol. 1*. New York, New York: Marvel Publishing, Inc., 2008.

Christiansen, Jeff, Mike Fichera, Stuart Vandal, Sean McQuaid, Michael Hoskin, Ronald Byrd, Markus Raymond, et al. *Official Handbook of the Marvel Universe A to Z Vol. 14*. New York, New York: Marvel Worldwide, Inc., 2010.

Christiansen, Jeff, Mike Fichera, Stuart Vandal, Sean McQuaid, Ronald Byrd, Mike O'Sullivan, Michael Hoskin, et al. *Official Handbook of the Marvel Universe A to Z Vol. 13*. New York, New York: Marvel Worldwide, Inc., 2010.

Christiansen, Jeff, Mike O'Sullivan, Sean McQuaid, David Wiltfong, Stuart Vandal, Ronald Byrd, Chad Anderson, et al. *Official Handbook of the Marvel Universe A to Z Vol. 4*. New York, New York: Marvel Worldwide, Inc., 2012.

Christiansen, Jeff, Mike O'Sullivan, Sean McQuaid, Michael Hoskin, Stuart Vandal, Ronald Byrd, David Wiltfong, et al. *Official Handbook of the Marvel Universe A to Z Vol. 5*. New York, New York: Marvel Worldwide, Inc., 2012.

Christiansen, Jeff, Mike O'Sullivan, Sean McQuaid, Stuart Vandal, Ronald Byrd, Michael Hoskin, Eric J. Moreels, et al. *Official Handbook of the Marvel Universe A to Z Vol. 3*. New York, New York: Marvel Worldwide, Inc., 2012.

Christiansen, Jeff, Sean McQuaid, Michael Hoskin, Stuart Vandal, Ronald

Byrd, David Wiltfong, Madison Carter, et al. *Official Handbook of the Marvel Universe A to Z Vol. 6*. New York, New York: Marvel Publishing, Inc., 2008.

Christiansen, Jeff, Sean McQuaid, Michael Hoskin, Stuart Vandal, Ronald Byrd, David Wiltfong, Madison Carter, et al. *Official Handbook of the Marvel Universe A to Z Vol. 7*. New York, New York: Marvel Publishing, Inc., 2009.

Christiansen, Jeff, Sean McQuaid, Michael Hoskin, Stuart Vandal, Ronald Byrd, David Wiltfong, Madison Carter, et al. *Official Handbook of the Marvel Universe A to Z Vol. 8*. New York, New York: Marvel Publishing, Inc., 2009.

Christiansen, Jeff, Sean McQuaid, Stuart Vandal, Ronald Byrd, Michael Hoskin, Mark O'English, Eric J. Moreels, et al. *Official Handbook of the Marvel Universe A to Z Vol. 2*. New York, New York: Marvel Publishing, Inc., 2008.

Christiansen, Jeff, Stuart Vandal, Sean McQuaid, Michael Hoskin, Mike O'Sullivan, Ronald Byrd, Mike Fichera, et al. *Official Handbook of the Marvel Universe A to Z Vol. 12*. New York, New York: Marvel Publishing, Inc., 2009.

Christiansen, Jeff, Stuart Vandal, Sean McQuaid, Michael Hoskin, Ronald Byrd, Mike Fichera, Madison Carter, et al. *Official Handbook of the Marvel Universe A to Z Vol. 9*. New York, New York: Marvel Publishing, Inc., 2009.

Christiansen, Jeff, Stuart Vandal, Sean McQuaid, Mike Fichera, Ronald Byrd, Michael Hoskin, Madison Carter, et al. *Official Handbook of the Marvel Universe A to Z Vol. 10*. New York, New York: Marvel Publishing, Inc., 2009.

Christiansen, Jeff, Stuart Vandal, Sean McQuaid, Ronald Byrd, Michael Hoskin, Mike Fichera, Mike O'Sullivan, et al. *Official Handbook of the Marvel Universe A to Z Vol. 11*. New York, New York: Marvel Publishing, Inc., 2009.

Couper-Smartt, Jonathan, Syd Barney-Hawke, Seth Biederman, and Kit Kiefer. *Marvel Encyclopedia Vol. 4: Spider-Man*. New York, New York: Marvel Comics, 2003.

DeFalco, Tom, and Matthew K Manning. *The Amazing Spider-Man: The Ultimate Guide*. London: Dorling Kindersley Limited, 2007.

DeFalco, Tom, Peter Sanderson, Tom Brevoort, Michael Teitelbaum, Daniel Wallace, Andrew Darling, and Matt Forbeck. *Marvel Encyclopedia*. London: Dorling Kindersley Limited, 2014.

Fingeroth, Danny. *A Marvelous Life: The Amazing Story of Stan Lee*. London: Simon & Schuster UK Ltd, 2019.

Fritz, Ben. *The Big Picture: The Fight for the Future of Movies*. Boston: Mariner Books, 2019.

Gruenwald, Mark, Eliot R Brown, Tom DeFalco, Mark Lerer, Peter Sanderson,

Danny Fingeroth, Steven Grant, et al. *The Official Handbook of the Marvel Universe*. New York, New York: Marvel Worldwide, Inc., 2019.

Hoskin, Michael, Anthony Flamini, Stuart Vandal, and Eric J Moreels. *Marvel Atlas*. New York, New York: Marvel Publishing, Inc., 2008.

Howe, Sean. *Marvel Comics: The Untold Story*. New York, New York: Harper, 2012.

Iger, Robert. *The Ride of a Lifetime*. London: Bantam Press, 2019.

Jensen, Daron, Al Sjoerdsma, Stuart Vandal, Paul Bourcier, Chris Buchner, Ronald Byrd, Russ Chappell, et al. *Captain America: Official Index to the Marvel Universe*. New York, New York: Marvel Worldwide, Inc., 2011.

Jensen, Daron, Al Sjoerdsma, Stuart Vandal, Paul Bourcier, Chris Buchner, Russ Chappell, Michael Hoskin, et al. *The Avengers: Official Index to the Marvel Universe*. New York, New York: Marvel Worldwide, Inc., 2011.

Jensen, Daron, Al Sjoerdsma, Stuart Vandal, Paul Bourcier, Chris Buchner, Russ Chappell, Michael Hoskin, et al. *Thor: Official Index to the Marvel Universe*. New York, New York: Marvel Worldwide, Inc., 2011.

Johnston, Jacob. *The Art of Captain America: Civil War*. New York, New York: Marvel Worldwide, Inc., 2016.

Johnston, Jacob. *The Art of Doctor Strange*. New York, New York: Marvel Worldwide, Inc., 2016.

Johnston, Jacob. *The Art of Guardians of the Galaxy Vol. 2*. New York, New York: Marvel Worldwide, Inc., 2017.

Jones, Nick. *Guardians of the Galaxy: The Ultimate Guide to the Cosmic Outlaws*. London: Dorling Kindersley Limited, 2017.

Meinerding, Ryan, Charlie Wen, Andy Park, Phil Saunders, Jackson Sze, Rodney Fuentebella, Anthony Francisco, Karla Ortiz, Adi Granov, and Troy Benjamin. *How to Paint Characters the Marvel Studios Way*. New York, New York: Marvel Worldwide, Inc., 2019.

O'Sullivan, Mike, Patrick Duke, Daron Jensen, Rob London, Chris Mccarver, Jacob Rougemont, and Kevin Wasser. *Marvel Cinematic Guidebook: The Good, The Bad, The Guardians*. New York, New York: Marvel Worldwide, Inc., 2017.

Roussos, Eleni. *The Art of Ant-Man and the Wasp*. New York, New York: Marvel Worldwide, Inc., 2018.

Roussos, Eleni. *The Art of Avengers: Endgame*. New York, New York: Marvel Worldwide, Inc., 2019.

Roussos, Eleni. *The Art of Avengers: Infinity War*. New York, New York: Marvel

Worldwide, Inc., 2018.

Roussos, Eleni. *The Art of Black Panther*. New York, New York: Marvel Worldwide, Inc., 2018.

Roussos, Eleni. *The Art of Captain Marvel*. New York, New York: Marvel Worldwide, Inc., 2018.

Roussos, Eleni. *The Art of Spider-Man: Far From Home*. New York, New York: Marvel Worldwide, Inc., 2019.

Roussos, Eleni. *The Art of Spider-Man: Homecoming*. New York, New York: Marvel Worldwide, Inc., 2017.

Roussos, Eleni. *The Art of Thor: Ragnarok*. New York, New York: Marvel Worldwide, Inc., 2017.

Roussos, Eleni. *The Movie Making Magic of Marvel Studios: Heroes & Villains*. New York, New York: Abrams Books for Young Readers, 2019.

Sjoerdsma, Al, Stuart Vandal, Chris Buchner, Ronald Byrd, Russ Chappell, Michael Hoskin, Daron Jensen, Jacob Rougemont, Robert J Sodaro, and Kevin Wasser. *The Amazing Spider-Man: Official Index to the Marvel Universe*. New York, New York: Marvel Worldwide, Inc., 2010.

Sjoerdsma, Al, Stuart Vandal, Michael Hoskin, Ronald Byrd, Daron Jensen, Chris Buchner, Jacob Rougemont, Russ Chappell, and Kevin Wasser. *Iron Man: Official Index to the Marvel Universe*. New York, New York: Marvel Worldwide, Inc., 2010.

Slack-Smith, Amanda. *Marvel: Creating the Cinematic Universe*. Brisbane, Queensland: Queensland Art Gallery | Gallery of Modern Art, 2017.

Smith, Dave. *Disney A to Z: The Official Encyclopedia (5th Edition)*. Glendale, California: Disney Editions, 2016.

Sumerak, Marc. *Guardians of the Galaxy: Creating Marvel's Spacefaring Super Heroes*. London: Titan Books, 2017.

Thomas, Roy. *75 Years of Marvel: From the Golden Age to the Silver Screen*. Cologne: Taschen GmbH, 2014.

Tucker, Reed. *Slugfest: Inside the Epic 50-Year Battle Between Marvel and DC*. London: Sphere, 2017.

Waid, Mark. *History of the Marvel Universe Treasury Edition*. New York, New York: Marvel Worldwide, Inc., 2019.

Wetzel, Stephanie, and Charlie Wetzel. *The Marvel Studios Story*. N.p.: HarperCollins Leadership, 2020.

Wiacek, Stephen. *Black Panther: The Ultimate Guide*. London: Dorling Kindersley Limited, 2018.

Wilkins, Jonathan, ed. *Marvel Studios: The First Ten Years*. London: Titan Magazines, 2018.

Magazines
Various articles, interviews, and reviews from the following magazines were used: *American Cinematographer, Backstory, Bloomberg Businessweek, Cinefix, Empire, Entertainment Weekly, FilmInk, SciFiNow, SFX, Total Film*, and *Wired*.

Podcasts
Episodes of the *Disney For Scores* podcast hosted by Jon Burlingame provided insight into how different composers have approached writing scores for the MCU.

The Empire Film Podcast spoiler specials focusing on the MCU movies were an indispensable source of behind-the-scenes information and points of clarification, with interviews being conducted with directors, producers, and actors.

Select episodes of Josh Horowitz's *Happy Sad Confused* podcast were also used for research.

Social Media
Facebook, Instagram, and Twitter posts by those who have been involved with the Marvel Cinematic Universe were sometimes consulted. Particularly insightful were tweets from James Gunn (@JamesGunn), Andy Park (@andyparkart), and the Russo brothers (@Russo_Brothers).

Websites
For interviews and news relating to a film's production I turned to CinemaBlend (cinemablend.com), Collider (collider.com), Comic Book Resources (comicbookresources.com), Deadline Hollywood (deadline.com), Den of Geek (denofgeek.com), Empire (empireonline.com), Entertainment Weekly (ew.com), The Hollywood Reporter (hollywoodreporter.com), HuffPost (huffpost.com), IGN (ign.com), NME (nme.com), Screen Australia (screenaustralia.gov.au), SuperHeroHype (superherohype.com), Syfy Wire (syfy.com), Uproxx (uproxx.com), Variety (variety.com), and Vulture (vulture.com).

"Jovial" Jay Shepard's MCU Location Scout articles over at RetroZap (retrozap.com/category/columns/mcu-location-scout/) were an invaluable resource for confirming much of my own research into the various filming locations used for the MCU. Movie-Locations.com (movie-locations.com) was also consulted.

Box office statistics were obtained from Box Office Mojo (boxofficemojo.com). Art of VFX (artofvfx.com) and fxguide (fxguide.com) were referred to for visual effects breakdowns. Specific articles from Set Decorators Society of America (setdecorators.org) were used for information on set decoration.

The Appendix to the Handbook of the Marvel Universe (marvunapp.com/Appendix/) and Marvel (marvel.com) were used for information pertaining to Marvel comic books.

PHOTO CREDITS

p. 15 - Atlanta, Georgia image by William Thompson.

p. 16 - The Victory Column image by kirillslov.

p. 30 - Patan Durbar Square image by Wolfgang Reindl.

p. 59 - Brandenburg Gate image by Nikolaus Bader.

p. 59 - *Spirit of America* image by skeeze.

p. 85 - Victoria Falls image by Albrecht Fietz.

p. 86 - Gwangan Bridge image by Sungho Song.

p. 103 - St Giles' Cathedral image by Eduardo Vieira.

p. 113 - San Francisco, California image by Free-Photos.

p. 163 - Charles Bridge image by Waldo Miguez.

p. 163 - Tower Bridge image by Phantaster.

All other images © Andy Thai

Image of Andy Thai with Stan Lee taken at Oz Comic-Con Melbourne in 2012

Andy Thai is a film fanatic and comic book geek from Sydney, Australia. Growing up, he was obsessed with Spider-Man and proudly owned Spider-Man socks, undies, t-shirts, video games, trading cards, and comic books. Spider-Man remains his favourite Marvel character to this very day.

ALSO AVAILABLE

AN UNOFFICIAL GUIDE TO THE
MARVEL CINEMATIC UNIVERSE

MARVELLOUS SYNERGY

PHASE TWO

Andy Thai

STAY CONNECTED

 facebook.com/**marvelloussynergy**
 instagram.com/**marvelloussynergy**
 marvelloussynergy.tumblr.com

Printed in the USA
CPSIA information can be obtained
at www.ICGtesting.com
LVHW011544291123
765067LV00004B/401